NEURAL NETWORKS IN C++

An Object-Oriented Framework for Building Connectionist Systems

Adam Blum

John Wiley & Sons, Inc.

New York ▪ Chichester ▪ Brisbane ▪ Toronto ▪ Singapore

To Jennifer

This publication is designed to provide accurate and authoritative information in regard to
the subject matter covered. It is sold with the understanding that the publisher is not en-
gaged in rendering legal, accounting, or other professional service. If legal advice or other
expert assistance is required, the services of a competent professional person should be
sought. FROM A DECLARATION OF PRINCIPLES JOINTLY ADOPTED BY A COM-
MITTEE OF THE AMERICAN BAR ASSOCIATION AND A COMMITTEE OF PUB-
LISHERS.

Library of Congress Cataloging-in-Publication Data
Blum, Adam
    Neural networks in C++ ; an object-oriented framework for building
  connectionist systems / Adam Blum.
      p.   cm.
    Includes bibliographical references and index.
    ISBN 0-471-55201-1 (book/disk set) – ISBN 0-471-53847-7 (pbk.)
    1. Neural networks (Computer science) 2. C++ (Computer program
  language) 3. Object-oriented programming.   I. Title.
QA76.87.358   1992
006.3–dc20   91-39648
                                                               CIP

Printed in the United States of America
10 9 8 7 6 5 4 3 2
Printed and bound by Malloy Lithographing, Inc.

About the Author

In his nine years of software development work, Adam Blum has been a principal contributor to several large software projects. These include a multidimensional spreadsheet interface for optimization problems, a language and compiler for authoring legal documents, and a new probabilistic method for text compression. He is now a senior software engineer with Phoenix Systems, a software development services company specializing in text and image retrieval applications, and electronic messaging system development. For Cambridge Information Group, he developed adaptive and probabilistic methods for various information retrieval problems including data compression, content-based indexing, and intelligent query formulation. He was employed for three years at IBM Federal Systems Division, working on, among other projects, systems to automate the design process of SDI. For another four years he developed software for Ketron Management Science, a leading provider of optimization software.

The author of several technical articles, Adam holds a BSCS from the University of Maryland–College Park and an MSCS from George Mason University. He is an active member of ACM, ACM SIGIR, ACM SIGART, and IEEE Computer Society. He lives with his wife, Jennifer, two cats, several C++ compilers, and a 486-33 in Falls Church, Virginia, a suburb of Washington, D.C. He believes in truth, justice, and the inevitable rise of C++ and parallel distributed solutions.

Contents

2

NEURAL NETWORK FUNDAMENTALS   35

3

NEURAL NET MODELS   51

4

APPLICATIONS OF NEURAL NETS 93

APPENDIXES

I

LISTINGS FOR NEURAL NET CLASS LIBRARY   127

II

LISTINGS FOR APPLICATIONS   181

REFERENCES   203

INDEX   209

Preface

Neural networks, which have received a lot of attention recently, are fascinating models of how our brains work, and they help to explain why our brains can do many things better than computers of conventional architecture. Books such as Rumelhart and McClelland's *Parallel Distributed Processing* [Rumelhart86] describe these models in detail and are stimulating reading for readers in a host of fields, from psychology to neurobiology to computer science. This book claims no such broad appeal, for we will not be looking at neural networks as a model of the brain's functioning. We will examine how a parallel distributed processing approach allows many types of problems to be solved much more easily than was previously possible with computers.

The book's intent is to appeal to programmers or, more accurately, people who implement computer solutions. This audience includes computer scientists, programmers, programmer analysts, and software developers—anyone looking for new methods and tools to apply to real-world problems.

One of the common indictments of artificial intelligence (AI) in general, and neural network research in particular, has been the lack of practical application of researchers' discoveries (which in many minds casts doubt on the validity of the research itself). This book should help to bridge the gap between theory and practical results in several ways. It will expose the fundamentals of neural net models to a broad class of practitioners. It will suggest application areas for these models and then present example applications in these areas. Finally, along the way to developing these example applications, a toolkit will be built to give the reader a basis for his or her own applications.

Other "stars" of this book are C++, and object-oriented programming (OOP) in general. C++ is rapidly becoming the standard for modern software development. It offers all the advantages of C, being (almost) completely downward compatible with ANSI C, and it provides many advantages over plain C. Chief of these advantages is its support for object-oriented programming. One of OOP's main advantages is (as will be expanded upon in this text) its ability to allow easy use of reusable tools. But the tools should already exist in order to be truly "reused."

In my first few neural net applications (which were actually done in C), I longed for some form of toolkit to ease the process so I could focus on the application instead of on the neural net implementation. The emergence of C++ helped somewhat. If any tools existed, they could be easily incorporated into a neural net application. Unfortunately, no such tools did exist at the time. At this writing C tools have begun to appear but there is still no C++ framework for neural net development. Frustrated with this state of affairs as I built neural net applications over the years, I attempted to encapsulate all the neural net portion into a set of reusable tools. One result was the publication in *Dr. Dobb's Journal* (in April 1990) of an implementation of the BAM System (an eminently useful model, as will be seen in the text). This book is a culmination of these efforts.

Neural networks have an incredible potential to advance the types of problems that are being solved by computers. Dozens of well-defined models exist that are readily applicable to some of the more difficult areas of computer applications. They just need to start being exploited. This book is one step in that direction. The rest, gentle reader, is up to you.

INTRODUCTION

Neural networks (NNs) are models of the brain's cognitive process. In contrast with conventional single-processor computers, the brain has a multiprocessor architecture that is highly interconnected. This architecture can be (and has been) described as *parallel distributed processing*. Parallel distributed processing has many advantages over single-processor models for many difficult computer science problems. It is one of the reasons that the brain, with its slow, error-prone individual hardware units (neurons) so outperforms even conventional supercomputers in some areas. Computer applications that use parallel distributed processing, or incorporate neural networks, allow problems that were once very difficult to solve on a computer to be attacked with relative ease.

In Chapter 1 we shall present the fundamentals of object-oriented programming, including a brief outline of the object-oriented framework used to develop our applications. In Chapter 2 we discuss the fundamentals of neural networks, including the formal model of a neuron, a summary of neuron activation functions, and various types of neural network learning. In Chapter 3 we present several neural network models and their implementations using our object-oriented framework. In Chapter 4 we apply the developed neural network implementations to several real-world problems. It is appropriate to begin these explorations with an elaboration of the history of neural networks and a discussion of the advantages neural networks offer for the solution of computer science problems.

■ HISTORY

Although this text is intended as a practical guide on how to apply neural networks to real-world problems, some discussion of the history of neural networks should be helpful. Neural networks originated as a model of how the brain works. Indeed, this research has its beginnings in psychology. The theories of Freud, William James, and other nineteenth-century psychologists laid the groundwork of ideas that was to give birth to early neural network research.

McCulloch and Pitts formulated the first neural network model [McCulloch 43]. It featured digital neurons but no ability to learn. The work of another psychologist, Donald Hebb, introduced the idea of Hebbian learning (as detailed in *Organization of Behavior* [Hebb 49]), which states that changes in synaptic strengths (connections between neurons) are proportional to the activations of the neurons. This was a formal basis for the creation of neural networks with the ability to learn.

The theory of Hebbian learning described a rule for updating synapse strengths in two-layer networks, enabling these networks to learn. Frank Rosenblatt incorporated this idea of learning into a two-layer network, calling the result a perceptron [Rosenblatt 57]. Rosenblatt formulated a learning rule based on weights adjusted in proportion to the error between output neurons and target outputs. His *perceptron convergence theorem* proved that this would result in a desired set of weights. Rosenblatt also formulated a three-layer perceptron and attempted to incorporate learning into it. However, he was unable to come up with a provably sound method of training the weights between the input and hidden-layer neurons.

Still, many problems cannot be solved with two-layer networks. The lack of a mathematically rigorous procedure to allow learning in multilayer networks was a major stumbling block to the development of neural network solutions. In 1969 Minsky and Papert mentioned this problem in *Perceptrons* [Minsky 69]. Minsky correctly pointed out the limitations of the perceptron for many problems and acknowledged the possibility that multilayer networks could overcome these limitations. But he did not see any way to enable these machines to learn, and so he felt that multilayer networks were a dead end.

Some interesting work continued to be performed within the bounds of two-layer networks. Kohonen used a two-layer network to build a content-addressable memory [Kohonen 84], in which no separate index must be given to retrieve a particular item; the item itself is the index. That is, instead of making a memory reference as $a[i]$, where a is the array and i is the index, to get to the contents c, we refer to the memory location as $a[c]$. Kohonen referred to this as *associative memory*. Associative memory is based on an unsupervised learning algorithm, where the weights are adjusted purely on the basis of the presented patterns, without regard to some desired output. In this book we will examine an extension of this concept, developed by Bart Kosko, known as *bidirectional associative memory* (BAM). Kohonen developed another unsupervised learning–based model known as the *learning vector quantizer* (LVQ). The LVQ uses competitive learning to allow input neurons to activate one and only one output neuron.

Since the mid-1960s Stephen Grossberg has been developing mathematical models of the brain's function [Grossberg 82]. The Center for Adaptive Systems is oriented to psychological and biological research. However, this research has resulted in several useful and unique neural network models, which are characterized by the ability to do training online, the capacity for self-organization, and the ability to form compact representations of complex phenomena. In addition, the "online training" aspect has allowed many of Grossberg's models (most prominently ART) to handle data that changes fundamentally over time. Specific models include the additive and multiplicative Grossberg models, the competitive learning concept just mentioned, adaptive resonance theory (ART), and various neural net–based minimal encoding methods, such as the outstar encoder. The outstar encoder was combined by Hecht-Nielsen with the Kohonen LVQ to form the counterpropagation model (which is used in this book).

Despite all the useful work occurring with two-layer systems, the independent discovery of backpropagation by Werbos in 1974 [Werbos 74] and Parker in 1982 [Parker 82] was the next major step in the advancement in neural nets, after Rosenblatt's perceptron. Backpropagation allows the training of multilayer networks. Thus the original objection that multilayer networks were a dead end because they could not be trained was removed. Werbos discovered it while working on his doctoral thesis in statistics, and he called the algorithm *dynamic feedback*. Parker discovered it independently in 1982 while doing graduate work at Stanford, and he called the algorithm *learning logic*. Rumelhart, Hinton, and Williams exploited backpropagation in 1986 in their work in simulating cognitive processes [Rumelhart, Hinton 86]. Their work was well broadcast throughout the scientific world through McClelland and Rumelhart's *Parallel Distributed Processing* [Rumelhart 86].

Since then backpropagation has been exploited in a number of fields having nothing to do with studying or simulating cognitive processes. It is a powerful and practical tool for solving problems that would be quite difficult using conventional computer science techniques. These problems range from image processing to speech recognition to character recognition forecasting to optimization. We will cover several of these application areas in this text.

Other models have been developed since then that offer advantages over the canonical backpropagation models for some applications. For example, in 1988 Bart Kosko introduced the BAM, an extension of Kohonen's attempts at content-addressable memory that allows two different types of patterns to be related, as opposed to the simpler auto-associator, where all patterns are of the same type [Kosko 88]. Both auto-associators and BAMs are plagued by capacity problems, and Kosko's BAM System approach (which can be extended to the associative memory system) of multiple layers of connectivity can be used to extend the capacity of these constructs.

Many of these models have begun to be implemented in VLSI (including the BAM). This is a particularly useful development. Many of the real-world benefits of these models cannot be realized without parallel hardware, and actually reducing the models to a chip is a step beyond that. Carver Mead is working on reproducing a complete nervous system in circuitry [Mead 89].

The progress in the adoption of neural networks as a problem-solving tool in the last few years is amazing. Disciplines that five years ago had not heard of neural networks now recognize NNs as the de facto best tool. Pick up a trade journal in the area of technical analysis of stocks and commodities, image recognition, or speech recognition, and note the number of ads and articles related to neural networks. However, the biggest advances are still to come, as the unique capabilities of neural networks are brought to bear on more and more difficult real-world problems.

■ ADVANTAGES OF NEURAL NETWORKS

For purely practical reasons, neural networks can do many things very well that are difficult to do with conventional single-processor solutions. This book presents applications in four areas: image recognition, forecasting, text retrieval, and optimization. All the applications benefit from the neural network approach to the difficult computer science problems contained therein.

One could argue that in each case it would be *possible* to formulate a statistical approach to the same problem. For example, in the image recognition applications, the program could make probabilistic guesses about what character is being viewed based on the results of a statistical model run prior to building the application. We could develop and run a statistical model to learn how to guess characters based on *known* features of each character's image. There are several problems with this approach, however, which is why progress in the fields of pattern recognition, voice recognition, handwriting recognition, and others was so slow prior to the advent of applied neural networks.

Less Need to Determine Relevant Factors a Priori

First, to formulate the statistical model we must know in general what factors we are trying to correlate. Neural networks excel at taking data presented to them and determining what data is relevant. Irrelevant data simply has such low connection strength to all of the output neurons that it results in no effect. In self-pruning networks, the data would be removed from the model altogether. The beauty is that we need never concern ourselves with just what input factors make a particular output result more likely. All we need to know is that it *works*.

This can *sometimes* be a disadvantage, however. There may be occasions when we need to verify the learned relationships directly. Later, we will discuss current efforts to build "knowledge extraction tools" for neural nets.

Sophistication of the Model

Model sophistication follows from the preceding point. Neural net models usually have literally hundreds of factors at play, some of which may have only a small effect. But the aggregate effect of all of these input factors is a model that is likely to be much more accurate for difficult problems than any statistical model we might formulate.

Directness of Model

A statistical model is simply a more indirect way of learning correlations. With a neural network approach, we model the problem directly. For example, if we are trying to map pixellated images to alphabetic characters, we literally connect the objects together. All pixels of the image are neurons and are connected (probably through at least one hidden layer) to the output neurons that identify the guessed character.

The alternative is the following circuitous route:

1. Determine what factors are likely to influence our guess of the character we're viewing.
2. Formulate a statistical model.
3. Run the model.
4. Analyze the results.
5. Build a system that incorporates these results (for example, one that makes a guess about characters based upon the most prominent statistical relationships between image features and characters).

Fault Tolerance

Because of the abundance of input factors, noise in the data or failure of some of the hardware is not as much of a problem with neural networks. In fact, we would generally want to train on noisy data, as this would probably enhance our post-training performance.

Inherent Parallelism

Each synapse in a neural net model can be its own processor. There are no time dependencies among synapses in the same layer; they may operate completely synchronously. Although many neural net implementations can run very successfully on single-processor machines (and all of the code in this book obviously is written to run on such a machine), this capability is not to be taken lightly.

Conventional single-processor machines are only so fast (the speed of light is a generally accepted upper bound for non-denizens of the starship Enterprise). Current efforts to speed up single-processor hardware center on making the hardware smaller (shortening the route that the electrons have to take). However, there is a lower bound to the size of our processors. We probably won't see processors smaller than individual molecules in the near future. We should probably not expect speedups of more than a couple orders of magnitude from current supercomputers, *given a single-processor machine.*

Makers of computer hardware certainly recognize this. The most recent Cray, at this writing, has four processors. The INMOS Transputer (a highly parallel machine) is readily available as an add-in board for several platforms. Even multiprocessor desktops (containing several 386s) are starting to appear. Several startup companies are building massively parallel "supermicros" with ganged i860s and i960s (both RISC chips from Intel). Intel itself is marketing the ETANN chip, which has 64 programmable processing elements, and the company provides hardware allowing this chip to be plugged into any 286-based or higher-level PC.

How do we as computer scientists exploit this hardware? In many problem areas, computer scientists are still trying to figure out ways to exploit vector processors (single instruction–multiple data, or SIMD), let alone parallel processors (multiple instruction–multiple data, MIMD). One approach is to build very smart compilers that will recognize possibilities for parallelism in sequential code and generate machine code accordingly. Indeed, many vendors of parallel hardware are funding such research in compiler technology. But the speedups as a result of this are not dramatic (rarely approaching an order of magnitude even for scientific applications), and processor usage in machines with more than a few processors is a very low percentage.

Even coding applications from scratch with parallelism in mind is extremely difficult. What algorithm do you use? Sure, you might be able to reduce a FOR loop to one cycle, but beyond optimizations of this type, what can you do? If you formulate a neural network solution to your problem—a "parallel distributed processing solution," if you will—the parallelism is built in and requires no tricks or difficult analysis.

Major advances in the types of problems that can be solved with computers will depend on the formulation of parallel distributed processing solutions. There are dozens of areas where conventional single-processor solutions have major weaknesses, and where applications can benefit from a neural network approach. We explore four areas in a very concrete way in this book. Many more exist, and many have not even been thought of yet.

1

THE OBJECT-ORIENTED FRAMEWORK

■ 1.1 INTRODUCTION TO OBJECT-ORIENTED PROGRAMMING

It was mentioned in the preface that a "star" of this book is object-oriented programming. This book should certainly appeal more strongly to those who already know what OOP is and how useful it can be. (Those of you in that category can skip ahead to Section 1.2, unless you already know C++, in which case you can skip ahead to Section 1.3.)

Object-oriented programming is characterized by many concepts: inheritance (single or multiple, preferably the latter), dynamic binding, polymorphism, and information hiding. These concepts overlap somewhat but are relatively easy to define (and we shall do so momentarily). It's a little bit harder to define OOP itself. OOP involves designing software around the "objects" in question. These objects are instances of "abstract data types" (a general OOP or software engineering term) or "classes" (the C++ handle for an abstract data type). An abstract data type is simply a definition of a complex data type *as well as* the "methods" that can act upon that data. Nothing can get at the data that constitutes an abstract data type without using the data type's methods.

Another way of defining OOP, for those who hate buzzwords, is just "data-centered design." Design the program around the data you will be acting on. It's unlikely that the fundamental data you are working with will change significantly. However, the functionality (what you do with that data) will be constantly enhanced and modified as time goes on. Typical structured programming techniques, such as "functional decomposition," concentrate on what a program *does,* rather than what it does it *to.* Such design methods require large-scale overhaul of the software when changes to the functionality are required (as they inevitably are).

There is a fair amount of jargon used in object-oriented programming. This should not be taken as a completely negative characteristic. Terms for various concepts in OOP give names to what otherwise might be somewhat amorphous ideas that would have to be fully explicated each time they were referred to. One unfortunate aspect of the current set of terminology is the inconsistency or redundancy of its application. In various areas, different terms are used to apply to the same concept, and (sometimes) the same term is used to apply to different concepts. One reason for this confusion is that different implementations of OOP languages (such as C++, SmallTalk, and Eiffel) use different names for identical things. One language's "member function" is another one's "method," for example.

We shall endeavor to keep our references to particular OOP concepts as consistent and nonredundant as possible in this book, avoiding the use of someone's pet name for an idea. With this in mind, we present brief definitions of major OOP concepts.

1.1.1 Class

A *class* may be described as an "abstract data type." It is an aggregation of related data elements together with all the "methods" that may operate on that data type to represent a unified concept. For a true abstract data type, the only access to the data itself is through the defined methods.

1.1.2 Object

An *object* is an instantiation of a class. Anything that is of the abstract data type that the class defines is an object. In a pure object-oriented program, we work only with objects. Our only function calls are messages to objects (or invocations of the objects' methods).

1.1.3 Information Hiding

Information hiding refers to the concept that our only access to the data in an abstract data type (or a class in C++ terminology) is through the "methods" defined in those classes. In fact, all of the data and methods have some attribute of information hiding associated with them. These attributes in C++ terminology are referred to as "public," "private," and "protected."

"Public" methods or data are available to any other class. Most methods are public. Exceptions are those methods that are used internally by the class to implement its public methods. Most data is not public, and there should be few exceptions to this rule. "Private" methods and data are available only to objects of the specified class. In general, all data used to represent an object of a particular class should be private. Private methods are used only to implement methods of the specified class. "Protected" methods or data are available only to objects of derived classes, where a derived class is a class that "inherits" its properties from a parent class.

Information hiding when used to maximum effect has several benefits: reliability, understandability, and, in some cases, efficiency. Software developed with information hiding tends to be more reliable since access to the data representation is restricted to those implementing the abstract data type. "Clients" of these abstract data types (developers using the code in their own applications) have no direct access to the data itself. Any actions on the data are taken through the controlled gateways of the class's methods, which presumably are written such that the integrity of the data is ensured. Once the methods are written and debugged, use of the class should be completely safe.

Understandability is enhanced since client developers need not understand the inner working of the class's methods or even the data representation of the object. The only thing a developer using the class needs to understand is the "class interface," or the set of methods available for that class. In a C++ program, this can be reduced to a procedure as simple as reading the method prototypes (not the actual fully coded methods) listed in the public section of a class definition in a header (.HPP) file. Of course, the developer also needs to know what each method requires to operate and what state the object is in after the method is called. It is important that the documentation for any class interface contain this information in a very accessible way. Bertrand Meyer has made this need for understanding "preconditions" and "postconditions" part of the language, in his excellent, very pure object-oriented language, Eiffel [Meyer 89].

Use of information hiding can actually enhance efficiency in object-oriented development. Making data accessible only in a few well-defined and indirect ways may actually make some programs more efficient than if the data were completely accessible. An example of this phenomenon is a pointer reference that might be publicly available in one class's data representation and private in another's. Certain compiler optimizations of pointer references that might be unsafe in generic C code or in C++ code where the pointer reference is not hidden or private can be performed with the version of the class that maximizes information hiding.

As another example, suppose an intelligent compiler can determine by analyzing the methods of a class that a particular part of the private section of a data representation is never used. It can simply be optimized away. This determination can be made at compile time (even before link time) because it can be determined simply from analyzing the source code. In C or in C++ with publicly available data, removal of unreferenced data is not possible until at least link time, and maybe not even then. This is an extreme example. In other cases, efficiency can be improved because all the ways in which a particular piece of data is going to be used are known exactly very early in the compile process.

1.1.4 Inheritance

Inheritance is the creation of a new class as an extension or specialization of an existing class. It allows the conceptual relationship between different classes to be made explicit. For example, the class *Apple* might be a descendant of the class *Fruit*. It is mostly identical to the class *Fruit,* but it may include some additional methods or data. Instead of duplicating the identical parts of the two classes, we can say that *Apple* "inherits" its definition from *Fruit*. In this case, only the additional methods and data need to be specified in the child class. Thus, inheritance allows not only easy comprehension of relationships between classes but also much easier construction of the classes themselves.

Inheritance also allows existing classes and class libraries to be easily modified to suit the job at hand. For example, with the toolkit presented here, if a class doesn't have all the necessary methods or if a modificaton to the model is needed, inheritance can be used to create a new class tailored to your needs. Inheritance enhances reusability of code, since existing code need not be modified at all. Existing classes can simply be inherited and the changes made to the derived class.

Inheritance may be single or multiple. *Single* inheritance implies obtaining characteristics from just one parent class. The preceeding example used single inheritance. *Multiple* inheritance obtains methods and data from multiple parent classes. An example might be an object of class *CircularWindow* that is derived from classes *Window* and *Circle*; it has available all the methods peculiar to circles as well as the methods appropriate to windows. In some early object-oriented languages (including early C++) only single inheritance was available. Modern C++ includes multiple inheritance, and in light of the state of modern OOP languages, it is reasonable to assume the availability of multiple inheritance.

Another characteristic of inheritance is the ability to treat objects of different classes as instances of the "generic" parent class. This allows us to handle groups of disparate objects as instances of a more uniform class. In fact, we can conceive of every class as being derived from the most generic class, Object (an extreme case that is not built into C++ and is not done in our class library). Some object-oriented environments (notably Smalltalk) and class libraries (notably the NIH class library [Gorlen 90]) actually assume this. A more realistic example might be a generic class called *Shape* that has several derived classes, such as *Rectangle, Triangle,* and *Circle*. These derived classes will share methods and characteristics of the data of the parent class. If we have a heterogeneous group of objects that share a parent class, we can treat it as a group of homogeneous objects of the parent class. This allows us to organize these objects as if they were of the same type. For example, we could group all the different *Rectangle, Triangle,* and *Circle* objects in a linked list of shapes. If we have the capability of sending identical commands to these differing objects, this feature is even more useful (see the following discussion of polymorphism).

While we are discussing the idea of generic classes, it is worth mentioning another type of "genericness" that does not involve inheritance. *Parameterized types* allow the creation of a class whose data representation can be changed as the need arises. For example, the vector class developed in our toolkit is a vector of floating-point numbers, but it might also be useful to have vectors of integers or vectors of bits. This is not easy to accomplish with inheritance if a base class already has the data representation. However, if the data representation could be "parameterized," we could have a generic class to which a parameter could be supplied to create specific classes for the different types of vectors. Currently, C++ has no such capability, so our toolkit does not have parameterized classes. However, this is a proposed enhancement to C++ referred to by Stroustrup as a "template" [Ellis 90]. The toolkit presented here could be easily modified (by making the vector class a template class) to take advantage of this new capability, once it exists in the language.

1.1.5 Virtual Functions and Abstract Classes

If the only purpose of a class is to be a parent for more specific derived classes, we may wish to have some methods in this base class be "virtual methods." In this case, if a pointer to the parent object invokes the method name and the object is actually of the derived class, the derived class method is invoked. For example, the class *Shape* may have a *draw* method that is defined (has some code associated with it) but is listed as "virtual." In this case, if the pointer is of class *Shape* but the actual instantiated object at run-time is of a derived class such as *Rectangle,* the *Rectangle draw* method will be invoked.

If we decide that a particular method will never be defined for a class, we can define the method as a "pure virtual" method, and no code will be associated with it. This makes the class an "abstract class." No object of an abstract class can ever be instantiated. Pointers may be of the class type, but they must actually refer to objects of derived classes. This will become clearer when we present the C++ mechanisms for defining virtual functions and abstract classes. The notion of an abstract class is especially powerful in conjunction with a system that lets us group disparate objects based on a common parent class (such as a linked list of shapes, where the individual shapes actually might be a circle, a triangle, and a rectangle) and send identical messages to each of the objects, which must each respond appropriately to them. For an example of an abstract class and inheritance, see Figure 1.1.

1.1.6 Polymorphism

The concept of sending different messages to different types of objects in object-oriented programming is referred to as *polymorphism*. Polymorphism allows us to send identical messages to different objects and have each object respond appropriately. We just mentioned an example where we might want to invoke methods on disparate objects with the same parent class. We may invoke a *display* method on each member of a linked list of shapes, the individual objects of which might be triangles, rectangles, and circles.

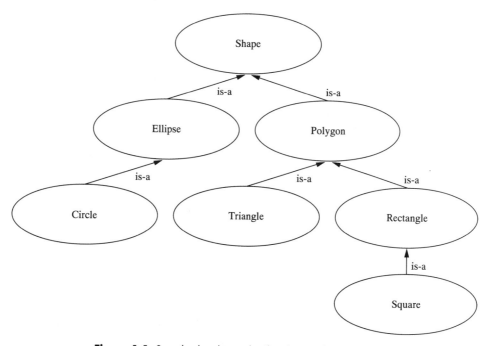

Figure 1.1 Sample class hierarchy (for abstract-shape example).

However, it is not necessary for the objects to be grouped or related for polymorphism to come into play. At the simplest level, two completely unrelated objects of two diffferent classes may each receive a *display* command, and each will respond to the command differently. In this case, polymorphism is required, but the specific code to be executed can actually be determined at compile-time. In the previous example, objects of several different classes were grouped together as a linked list of pointers to objects of the parent class. The linked list might be built dynamically, in which case we would not know at compile-time what specific code would be executed for the *display* method. This would have to be determined on the fly at run-time for each invocation of a method on any element of the linked list.

Often when polymorphism is mentioned, this is the phenomenon that is referred to. This definition of polymorphism is a bit stricter, implying the capability to send different commands to different objects that are grouped as heterogeneous collections of descendants of a common base class. Under this definition, it is the combination of inheritance and the ability to determine the actual code at run-time (*dynamic binding,* which we shall define momentarily) that enables us to perform polymorphism.

We do not use this strict definition of polymorphism here. This capability is very powerful, and often handy. However, it entails a high cost in performance. Each method invocation requires a far call (machine instruction) to look up the actual function and another far call to execute it. We try to avoid this in our library. However, we do want different objects to share common interfaces. This phenomenon is also referred to as *polymorphism,* especially in compiled object-oriented languages, where dynamic binding is often avoided where possible [Stroustrup, Ellis 90]. However, dynamic binding is certainly a powerful tool that should be discussed here.

1.1.7 Dynamic Binding

Dynamic binding may also be referred to as "late binding" because the method is not bound to specific code until as late as possible (when the method is invoked at run-time). Dynamic binding requires that a "method table" be maintained during execution. When the *display* method is called for an object, the class of the object is determined first. Then the actual function to be executed for the method is determined by looking up the method name and class identifier in the method table. Thus, with dynamic binding we incur not just the overhead of the function call when invoking a method, but also the expense of the method lookup. It is certainly a powerful capability that must be provided in an object-oriented environment, yet it should be avoided in portions of the code where performance is critical.

In our toolkit, as far as possible, objects have common interfaces in method names and arguments. Inheritance is also used wherever possible to make the relatedness of different objects more explicit and to simplify the creation of new objects. Dynamic binding is avoided in our toolkit for reasons of performance and because it is not essential to any of the implementations. However, as you extend your toolkit to new applications, you may find a context where it becomes useful. For example, if you build an application that uses several of the neural network models implemented in the toolkit, you may want to refer to specific instances of a neural network model (for example, a backprop net) with a pointer to the abstract base class (*net*). If you then invoke one of *net*'s methods on the pointer, such as *train,* the application will determine at run-time which of the many possible train functions will be called.

Many programmers (including perhaps those who have not even explicitly used an OOP language) will say, "But I already do it that way." That's great. But it's much more difficult to do OOP design and programming in "conventional" languages, which even at their best are tailored to "structured design," which, as mentioned, is in many ways the opposite of OOP. If you want to do OOP, the best way to go is to use a language designed for it, such as C++.

■ 1.2 INTRODUCTION TO C++

C++ was invented by Bjarne Stroustrup of AT&T Bell Labs. Dr. Stroustrup was an enthusiastic user of Simula, a simulation language that had many object-oriented capabilities. When it became necessary for him to write projects in C, he missed the abstract data types and other OOP features from Simula. So he created "C with Classes," which came to be known as C++.

C++ can be viewed as just that: C with classes. A *class* is the C++ (and Simula) term for an abstract data type. Of course, C already has a way of aggregating data into a complex type—the *struct*. A class is a struct with a few more features. First, part of the data (preferably all of it) can be kept "private," with the only access to this data through the "methods" associated with the class. A *method* is just a C function, but it is bound to a particular class and has access to all of the class's data. (A class that is entirely "public" is the same thing as a struct and in fact can be defined as a struct.)

Classes also have the capability of inheritance. The programmer can "inherit" all of the data, and methods, of another class and add what is needed. This is particularly useful for code reuse (which, it is hoped, will occur with this book). In C and other conventional languages, if some code does not meet our needs, we at the least must modify the code. Inheritance allows us to take an existing class and augment or modify it as necessary. In fact, a C++ class has the capability of "multiple inheritance": a class can inherit data from more than one other class.

We've mentioned C++'s capabilities in broad overview, presenting no syntax. Before we get specific, it is appropriate to mention the background in programming that is assumed here. We assume the reader is familiar with some programming language, preferably C. After all, quite a bit of code will be presented here, and this is a practitioner's guide. However, we don't assume you are a C++ expert. Some awareness of the language and its capabilities is helpful, but C++ is a young language and we do not expect you to know C++ before reading this.

If you are interested in further reading on C++, an excellent reference is Ellis and Stroustrup's *Annotated C++ Reference Manual* (the *ARM*) [Ellis 90]. The *ARM*, however, is not meant as a gentle introduction. Lippman's *C++ Primer*, now in its second edition, is also superb [Lippman 91]. Other good texts are Eckel's *Using C++* [Eckel 89] and Dewhurst and Stark's *Programming in C++* [Dewhurst 89]. Note that all of these books cover at least C++ 2.0 (Lippman's covers 3.0). Many (earlier) C++ books don't, and you should avoid them. C++ 2.0 has many significant features, multiple inheritance and a new streams library being most prominent. This book *will* use these capabilities. AT&T has released version 3.0 of the language, but this is not covered in the *ARM*, which is the ANSI base document. It is likely that a forthcoming ANSI standard for C++ will be based on C++ 2.0. Features specific to AT&T release 3.0 are not used.

There is also the issue of the C++ compilers themselves. We will use code that compiles with Zortech's C++ 2.1 compiler and Borland's *Borland* C++ 2.0 (a follow-on to Borland's Turbo C++ 1.0). By the time this book is published, Microsoft's C++ compiler should be available, and all code will be compilable with this as well. Although the compilers mentioned are PC compilers, "PCisms" will be avoided. Also, any run-time library calls will be restricted to the ANSI C standard library (which can be assumed to be present in any conformant C++ environment). Unfortunately, there is no ANSI standard C++ class library. Any of the class library extensions provided with the compilers mentioned are therefore avoided. Any C++ compiler that is compliant with AT&T C++ 2.0 should handle all the code with minimal changes.

1.2.1 Appropriateness to Neural Network Development

When we create a class in C++, we can also "overload operators" to apply to that class. This allows us to create a higher-level programming vocabulary. For example, with regard to vectors and matrices, which will be very important in implementing neural nets, we can overload arithmetic operators to work with whole vectors and matrices at a time. We can code A+B to add two matrices instead of using a lot of hard-to-follow code. This makes C++ an excellent presentation method for explaining algorithms. We can then dispense with pseudocode, which is of questionable value in a practitioner's guide anyway. The pseudocode is the code itself. The code is presented in the same vocabulary as the theory.

Also, as we create different types of neural networks (which will each have their own class), we will use the same method names for all the things we need the neural net to do: methods to *encode* a pattern association, *recall* an output pattern, *train* themselves, and *run* themselves. C++'s polymorphism allows us to use the same method call for each type of neural net object. If we change the type of neural network used to implement a particular application, we need only change the declaration of the neural network object. All the rest of the code will remain the same.

■ 1.3 BASIC OBJECTS IN CONNECTIONIST SYSTEMS

We have talked about object-oriented programming in general, but we have not yet described the actual neural net models we will be implementing. However, we do know the common components of these models: layers of neurons and synapses. At the lowest level, fields of neurons are represented as vectors, and synapses (the connections between these fields of neurons) are represented as matrices. Classes for vectors and matrices should greatly facilitate the implementation of neural nets.

Thus, as a first step, we want to have classes for matrices and vectors so that our implementations of neural net models can build on them. Although several commercial libraries providing matrix and vector classes have appeared, not all of the methods available in these libraries are necessary for our applications, and many that are necessary are not available. Also, a major purpose of this book is to show *how to build* software using object-oriented tools. So we will build matrix and vector classes tailored and optimized for neural network programming as we go. For a diagram of these basic objects, see Figure 1.2.

1.3.1 The Vector Class

In writing a class we need to determine two things: (1) how to represent our data and (2) what we need to do with it. For vectors, the first decision

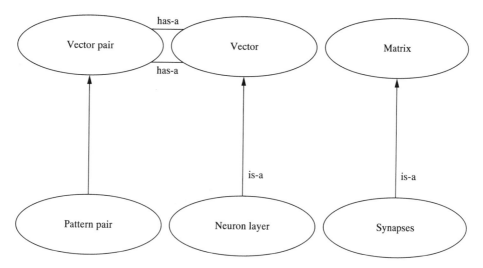

Figure 1.2 Basic objects classs hierarchy.

is reasonably straightforward. We need an array of numbers. In most of the neural nets we will build, these need to be floating-point numbers. Some nets may just use integers or even individual bits, but since we don't want to write several vector classes, we will use floating-point vectors as a "worst case" that can handle any type of vector we need to represent. Unfortunately, there is no standard method built into C++ for parameterized data types. "Templates" for data types have been proposed but have not found their way into most implementations. Thus, the common method is to use the C preprocessor, but this is a clumsy method and not appropriate for an explanatory text. We must be able to handle an array of numbers of any size, so we need to represent it as a pointer to a floating-point number, with an integer representing the size of the array. This gives us our data representation for a vector.

The class definition for *vec* follows as listing 1.1. Remember, a class is just like a C struct except that it has both public and private sections and ca have methods or functions associated with it. The private section (above t keyword *public,* the keyword *private* is assumed but could be placed there i desired) has just two data elements: the size indicator, int n, and a pointer to an array of floating points, double *v (ignore the "friend" statements for now). The classes presented here in the text are abbreviated versions actually meant to convey the substance of the class rather than all its details. Please see the appendices or the accompanying source code (in .HPP header files) for the full presentations of class definitions.

What things do we need to do with vectors? Every class needs a way of creating and destroying objects, so a class will generally have both a constructor and a destructor. The *vec* constructor takes arguments of size and an initialization value. Both of these arguments have a default that takes effect if the argument is left out in the call; for size it is MAXVEC (a defined constant), and for value it is zero.

Beyond the destructor and constructor, a host of arithmetic operators are provided. In the definition we use syntax such as operator+, but the operators may be used without explicit use of the word *operator*. For example, if we have two objects of the *vec* class, A and B, we can add them with A + B.

We would also like to be able to input and output vectors easily. C++ has its own I/O library called *streams*, and input and output can be invoked using the >> and << operators. However, we need to give these operators (which we will have to write for the vector class) access to the internals of our *vec* class. We do this by saying that these operators are "friends" and can have access to the internals of *vec*. This explains the two "friend" statements at the top of the class definition. We may also want entire classes to be "friends" of *vec*. We give the matrix class access to *vec* with the "friend class matrix" statement.

There are other methods provided—*maxindex, distance, normalize* (presented in the full definition of the classes), and so on. The value of these will not become clear until we implement specific neural nets, so we will not explain them now.

The following vector class definition would generally be included in any module that uses the *vec* class. Note that we have only the declarations of the methods or functions associated with *vec*. We generally do not *define* the function (code it) in the class definition (unless it is very small). The definition of functions is generally done in a source (.CPP) file. Each function is prefaced by the class name followed by a double colon (::) and the method name. For example, the *vec* length method might be defined as `int vec::length(){return n;}`.

Listing 1.1: The Vector Class

```
// an abbreviated version of the vector class definition

class vec {

        friend istream& operator>>(istream& s,vec& v1); friend ostream&
        operator<<(ostream& s,vec& v1);

                int n;
                double *v;

        public:
                vec(int size=MAXVEC,int val=0); // constructor
                ~vec(); // destructor
                vec(vec &v1); // copy initializer

                int length();

                vec& operator=(const vec& v1); // vector assignment
                vec operator+(const vec& v1); // vector addition
                vec operator-(const vec& v1);
                vec& operator+=(const vec& v1); // vector add assignment
                double operator*(const vec& v1); // dot-product
                vec operator*(double c); // multiply by constant
                vec& operator* =(double c); // vector multiply by constant
                // vector transpose multiply needs access to v array
                int operator==(const vec& v1);
                double operator[](int x);

}; // vector class
```

1.3.2 The Matrix Class

We also need matrices to represent the synapses between layers of neurons. The matrix class is implemented as an array of pointers (int **) with indicators of the number of rows and columns. These are made protected instead of private to allow classes derived from a matrix to have access to the internal data. The matrix class could conceivably have been implemented as an array of vector objects. This representation was chosen for efficiency.

Several constructors are provided. The first simply initializes the matrix from specified dimensions. These dimensions default to the particular application's two pattern lengths (specified by the ROWS and COLS constants). Other constructors are provided to form a matrix from a pair of vectors by multiplying one vector by the transpose of another ($\mathbf{M} = \mathbf{AB}^T$). Standard matrix arithmetic functions are included. Methods are also provided to form a vector from a row or column "slice" of the matrix, or to insert rows or columns to the matrix from a vector. Streams output is provided for debugging diagnostics.

Listing 1.2: The Matrix Class

```
// an abbreviated version of the matrix class definition

class matrix {
        friend ostream& operator<<(ostream& s,matrix& m1);
        friend istream& operator>>(istream& s,matrix& m1);
        protected:
                double **m; // the matrix representation
                int r,c; // numbers of rows and columns
        public:
                // constructors
                matrix(int n=ROWS,int p=COLS,double range=0);
                ~matrix();
                int depth();
                int width();
                matrix& operator=(const matrix& m1);
                matrix& operator+(const matrix& m1);
                matrix& operator+=(const matrix& m1);
vec operator*(vec& v1);
}; // matrix class
```

1.3.3 The Vector Pair Class

The final class we need is the vector pair class. This may seem to be a somewhat artificial construct. But remember, what neural networks do is learn associations between patterns (represented as vectors), so vector pairs will be fundamental to many of our neural net implementations. An *encode* operation may encode a vector pair, and a *recall* operation may return a vector pair when supplied with a pattern (or *vec*).

The vector pair is represented by just two vector objects. Methods are provided for assignment and testing for equivalence.

```
class vecpair {
        friend istream& operator>>(istream& s,vecpair& v1);
        friend ostream& operator<<(ostream& s,vecpair& v1);
        friend matrix::matrix(const vecpair& vp);
              int flag; // flag signaling whether encoding succeeded
        public:
              vec *a,*b;
              vecpair(int n=ROWS,int p=COLS); // constructor
              vecpair(const vec& A,const vec& B);
              vecpair(const vecpair& AB); // copy initializer

              ~vecpair();
              vecpair& operator=(const vecpair& v1);
              int operator==(const vecpair& v1);
```

However, layers of neurons are more than just vectors, and matrices of synapses are more than just matrices. We will use inheritance to allow neuron layers to "inherit" vectors and add other things as necessary. Matrices of synapses will generally just be part of any neural net object we create, so inheritance may not be necessary. In other words, a layer of neurons *is a* vector (plus some more stuff), and a particular neural net *has a* matrix of synapses. Such determinations of whether a relationship is "is-a" or "has-a" are often faced in object-oriented design. Given that we have to create an object that might need aspects of another object, we can say that the object either contains the other object (has-a) or is derived from another object (is-a). This will become clearer as we develop the architecture for our neural network toolkit.

1.3.4 The Neural Network Class

Besides the capability of using vectors and matrices to represent layers of neurons and matrices of synapses, there are other actions that all the neural networks presented here need to perform. They all need to be trained from a set of available facts, they all need to be tested from another set of facts (not included in the training process), and they all need to be run on a set of inputs once they have been trained and tested.

The presented networks also share characteristics of data. They all have sizes specified for the input pattern presented and the output pattern recalled. Some networks, notably auto-associators, might not have an explicit output pattern (input patterns feed back and modify themselves); however, none of the models presented are auto-associative. Anyway, this can be handled by having the output pattern be the changed input pattern. The input and output patterns themselves are arguments to the *encode* and *recall* methods; they are not intrinsic parts of the neural network data representation. There are also parts of the common neural network data representation for learning rate, decay, and tolerance. Learning rate modulates the degree to which an individual fact changes the weight. Decay rate indicates the extent to which a weight may decay over a time period. Tolerance indicates the degree to which we will accept errors in predicted output patterns before we pronounce the network "trained." (In the beginning of the next chapter, we will define these concepts in detail.)

Next we define a class called *net* that each of our networks will use. It has methods declared *and defined* for *train, cycle, test,* and *run.* The *train* method will run on a set of presented facts until the desired tolerance is reached. It allows the training to be either suspended and continued at a later time or simply suspended if learning fails to fall within the specified tolerance. Each of these methods may be invoked by objects of child classes. The hidden methods *saveweights* and *loadweights* are used to effect this save-and-restart capability. The *train* method also uses the *cycle* method, which makes one pass through the entire set of facts and invokes the *encode* operation on each fact.

A constructor method is also available for the class, even though it is an abstract class and will never have an object instantiated. The constructor method is used to set the values of data in the class's private section. It will be used by the constructors of child methods to initialize the data of the parent class. Although it may seem strange to have a constructor for an abstract class, it is far better than having each derived class repeat the code necessary to initialize the parent class. The constructor reads the values for each parameter from a definition file (with the .DEF extension). Several possible parameters may be specified in a definition file by listing the name of the parameter followed by its value. If the parameter is not listed in the definition file, it remains at the default. For the generic neural network, there are five named parameters: INPUTS, OUTPUTS, DECAY, RATE, and TOLERANCE. INPUTS specifies the number of neurons in an input pattern, OUTPUTS the size of the output pattern, DECAY the rate of weight decay, RATE the learning rate, and TOLERANCE the degree to which predictions can deviate from the output patterns. Specific neural networks may have many more patterns in addition to these.

Also declared (but not defined) are some pure virtual functions, those specified as "equal to zero": *encode* and *recall. Encode* takes an input-output "fact" in the form of a vector pair and stores it in the network. *Recall* takes an input (represented as a vector) and returns an output (in the form of another vector). The existence of these pure virtual methods makes the neural network class an abstract class; no actual instantiations of it will exist. But each of the neural network models presented is derived from it (albeit in some cases through multiple inheritance). The top-level functionality available is the same for each of the neural network models. However, the lower-level (but still public) methods will differ in their implementations, although their interfaces are identical.

The abstract base class enhances the consistency of the presented applications, makes the generic operation of neural networks more understandable, and allows only the unique aspects of a particular neural network model to be presented, with the common features inherited from the generic class.

```
class net {
private:
        char *name;   // string used as base name for files
        int n; // size of input layer
        int p; // size of output layer
        int cycleno; // keep track of which cycle during training
        float learnrate; // learning rate (defined as 1 where not gradual)
        float decay;     // decay (default constructed as
        // zero if not applicable)
        float tolerance; // how close to output prediction must be

        // private methods used to store and retrieve weights during
        // training process
        int saveweights();
        int loadweights();

public:
        // used by constructor to read in parameters
        enum parmtype={inputs,outputs,rate,decay,tolerance};

        net(char *s);
        ~net();

        // pure virtual encode and recall functions make this
        // class abstract
        virtual void encode(vecpair& v) = 0; //
        virtual vec recall(vec& v) = 0;

        virtual float cycle(ifstream& s);
        virtual void train();
        virtual float test();    // floating point-value indicates
        //percentage correct of test
        virtual void run();
};
```

■ 1.4 CLASS HIERARCHY

To make this discussion clearer, let us present the initial object architecture of our toolkit (See Figure 1.3). This architecture is often referred to as a *class hierarchy*. Traditionally, a class hierarchy depicts the inheritance structure of a group of classes (presumably related classes, or there would be no hierarchy to depict). In the class hierarchy diagrams, each class is shown as a node in a directed graph, where an edge indicates that a class is derived from another class. By convention, we will depict the parent class on the end of the edge with the arrow. This also corresponds somewhat to the way inheritance is performed in C++. The child class indicates that it inherits everything from a parent class (or a number of parent classes). In effect, it "points" to a parent class.

This is the traditional sense of a class hierarchy. But there is actually a lot more information we may want to know about how classes are related. As

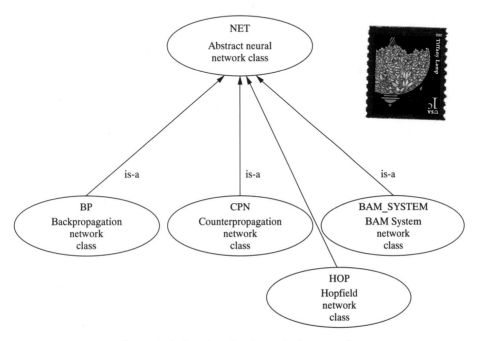

Figure 1.3 Complete class hierarchy for our toolkit.

already mentioned, there are "is-a" and "has-a" relationships. Class hierarchies traditionally depict the inheritance structure—the "is-a" relationships. However, we may also want to see the "has-a" relationships. These are depicted by showing one class containing another. (The hierarchy presented in Figure 1.3 is only for the toolkit including the abstract neural network class, not for any specific neural network classes. The class hierarchies for these will be presented in Chapter 3.)

These two constructs, along with the generic neural net class, form the building blocks of our neural net models. It may be a little premature to present them here, but they will provide a roadmap for our discussion of the individual models in the following chapters, and they should be referred back to while you read the text. In developing object-oriented software, it is useful to always have a class hierarchy diagram available. You should keep this in mind when making your own extensions to this hierarchy.

2

NEURAL NETWORK FUNDAMENTALS

■ 2.1 MODEL OF A NEURON

We will present various neural network models in this chapter. First, though, we should define their fundamental building block, the neuron.

The neuron is the basic processor in neural networks. Each neuron has one output, which is generally related to the state of the neuron—its activation— and which may fan out to several other neurons. Each neuron receives several inputs over these connections, called synapses. The inputs are the activations of the incoming neurons multiplied by the weights of the synapses. The activation of the neuron is computed by applying a *threshold function* to this product. An abstract model of the neuron is shown in Figure 2.1.

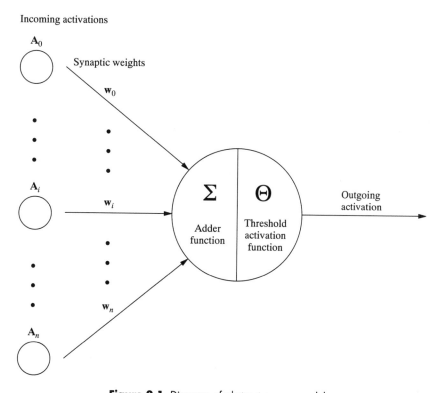

Figure 2.1 Diagram of abstract neuron model.

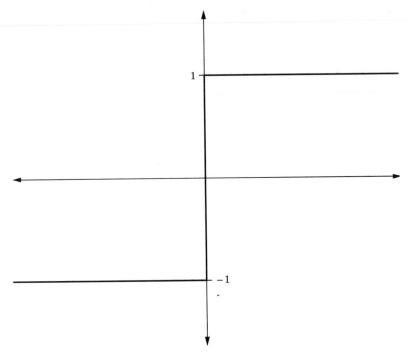

Figure 2.2 Figure of step function.

■ 2.2 ACTIVATION FUNCTIONS

This threshold function is generally some form of nonlinear function. One simple nonlinear function that is appropriate for discrete neural nets is the step function (Figure 2.2). One variant of the step function is:

$$f(x) = \begin{cases} 1 & \text{if } x > 0 \\ f'(x) & \text{if } x = 0, \quad \text{where } f'(x) \text{ refers to the previous value of } f(x) \\ & \qquad \text{(that is, the activation of the neuron} \\ & \qquad \text{will not change)} \\ -1 & \text{if } x < 0 \end{cases}$$

where x is the summation (over all the incoming neurons) of the product of the incoming neuron's activation and the synaptic weight of the connection:

$$x = \sum_{i=0}^{n} A_i w_i$$

where n is the number of incoming neurons, A is the vector of incoming neurons, and w is the vector of synaptic weights connecting the incoming neurons to the neurons we are examining.

Another popular class of function, one more appropriate to analog nets, is the sigmoid, or squashing, functions. An example is the logistic function illustrated in Figure 2.3:

$$f(x) = \frac{1}{1 + e^{-x}}$$

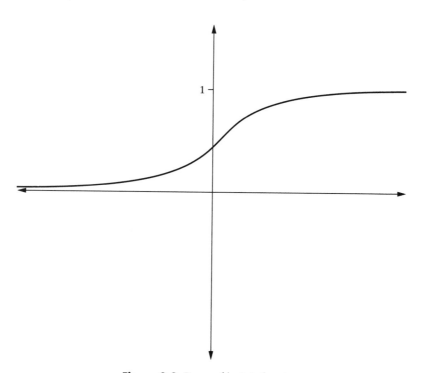

Figure 2.3 Figure of logistic function.

Other sigmoid functions are available. Another popular alternative is:

$$f(x) = \tanh(x)$$

The most important characteristic of our activation function is that it be non-linear. If we wish to use an activation function in a multilayer network, the activation function must be nonlinear, or the computational power will be equivalent to a single-layer network (we will not be able to learn nonlinear mappings).

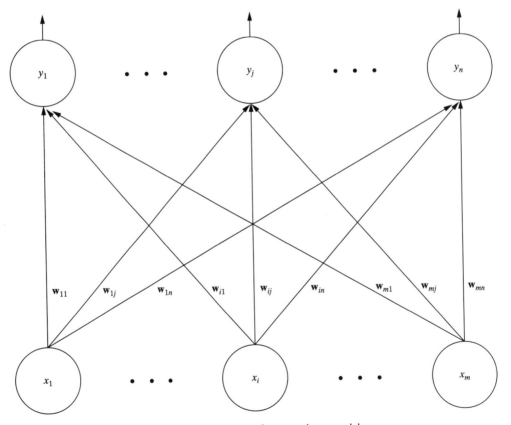

Figure 2.4 Diagram of synapse layer model.

■ 2.3 LEARNING

All of the "knowledge" that a neural network possesses is stored in the "synapses," the weights of the connections between the neurons (Figure 2.4). Earlier we mentioned that the synapses between two layers of neurons would be represented as matrices.

Once the knowledge is present in the synaptic weights of the network, presenting a pattern for input to the network will produce the correct output. However, how does the network acquire that knowledge? This happens during "training." Pattern associations are presented to the network in sequence, and the weights are adjusted to capture this knowledge. The weight adjustment scheme is known as the *learning law.*

One of the first learning methods formulated was Hebbian learning. Donald Hebb, in his *Organization of Behavior* [Hebb 49] formulated the concept of "correlation learning." This is the idea that the weight of a connection is adjusted based on the values of the neurons it connects:

$$\Delta \mathbf{w}_{ij} = \alpha a_i a_j$$

where α is the learning rate, a_i is the activation of the ith neuron in one neuron layer, a_j is the activation of the jth neuron in another layer, and $\mathbf{w}_{ij}$ is the connection strength between the two neurons. A variant of this learning rule is the signal Hebbian law:

$$\Delta \mathbf{w}_{ij} = -\mathbf{w}_{ij} + S(a_i)S(a_j)$$

where S is a sigmoid function.

2.3.1 Unsupervised Learning

Since the learning method just described does not test the resultant weights to see if they yield acceptable outputs, this method is described as an *unsupervised learning method.* In general, an unsupervised learning method is one in which weight adjustments are not made based on comparison with some target output. There is no "teaching signal" feed into the weight adjustments. This property is also known as *self-organization.*

Two examples of unsupervised learning that are presented here are *additive matrix* learning, exemplified by the BAM and BAM System, and the *learning vector quantizer* component of the counterpropagation (these models will be discussed in detail in the next chapter). Additive matrix learning in BAM is similar to the Hebbian formula just presented but is even simpler since the weight changes are not modulated by a learning rate or a sigmoid function. The weights are changed by adding the matrix resulting from the product of the input and output vectors to the existing matrix. The learning vector quantizer is an example of a different kind of unsupervised learning. It is a "nearest-neighbor classifier." Based on the input pattern, one (or sometimes a few) output neuron is chosen as the "winner," and only the weights to the winning neuron are adjusted.

2.3.2 Supervised Learning

In many models learning takes the form of supervised training. We present input patterns one after the other to the neural net and observe the recalled output pattern in comparison with our desired result. We then need some way of adjusting the weights that takes into account any error in the output pattern. An example of a supervised learning law is the *error correction law*:

$$\Delta \mathbf{w}_{ij} = \alpha a_i [c_j - b_j]$$

where α is again the learning rate, a_i is the activation of the ith neuron and b_j the activation of the jth neuron in the recalled pattern, and c_j is the desired activation of the jth neuron.

2.3.3 Reinforcement Learning

Another learning method, known as *reinforcement learning* fits into the general category of supervised learning, but its formula differs from the error correction formula just presented. This type of learning is similar to supervised learning except that each output neuron gets an error value, and only one error value is computed for each output neuron. The weight adjustment formula is then:

$$\Delta \mathbf{w}_{ij} = \alpha(v - \Theta_j)e_{ij}$$

where α is again the learning rate, v is the single value indicating the total error of the output pattern, and Θ_j is the threshold value for the jth output neuron. We need to spread out this "generalized" error for the jth output neuron to each of the incoming i neurons. e_{ij} is a value representing the eligibility of a weight for updating. This may be computed as

$$e_{ij} = \frac{d \ln g_i}{d \mathbf{w}_{ij}}$$

where g_i is the probability of the output being correct given the input from the ith incoming neuron. (This is a vague description; the probability function is of necessity a heuristic estimate and manifests itself differently from specific model to specific model.)

However, the error correction algorithm can be viewed as just a specific example of this generalized reinforcement learning, where the "spreading" of the error over the i incoming neurons is done by the activation of the incoming neuron itself. Instead of using a more global estimate of the error, the error correction rule uses the specific error on the jth output neuron. The eligibility of a weight for updating in the simple error correction rule presented here is based only on the activation of the input-layer neuron. Also, our error correction law does not depend at all on the changes of a weight during the previous update, as the reinforcement law does. This may be considered the salient innovation of reinforcement learning.

■ 2.4 MULTILAYER NETWORKS

Earlier we discussed how two-layer perceptrons were limited in their ability to learn nonlinear mappings—relationships between input and output patterns. A very simple example of this is the exclusive-OR problem. In this problem, we want to have our simple two-layer network learn the pattern association depicted in Figure 2.5.

For problems such as this that require classification, the two-layer network can classify only functions that are *linearly separable.* Linear separability implies that a hyperplane of $n - 1$ (where n is the number of input factors) dimensions can be constructed that divides the regions for the different classes. This cannot be done for the exclusive-OR function, as can be seen in Figure 2.6. In Figure 2.6 (with just two dimensions), linear separability translates into the ability to draw a line separating the two classes. No set of synaptic weights in a two-layer network will result in the desired outputs given each input pattern. But suppose we could add a third dimension to our graph, and the value in the third dimension is 1 only if both inputs are 1, and it is 0 otherwise. Then, as seen in Figure 2.7, a plane can be drawn that separates the points.

If we construct a neural net with an additional layer of neurons between the input and output layers, we can achieve the same result (Figure 2.8). We refer to this additional layer as a "hidden layer" since it does not interact directly with the outside layer. The neurons that receive input from the outside world make up the input layer, and the neurons that receive inputs from hidden-layer

Input	Output
0 0	0
0 1	1
1 0	1
1 1	0

Figure 2.5 Mapping for XOR problem.

Figure 2.6 XOR problem in two dimensions.

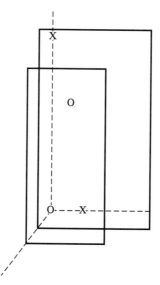

Figure 2.7 Three dimensional representation of XOR problem.

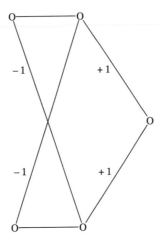

Figure 2.8 Three layer
network that emulates
the XOR function.

neurons and create outputs visible to the outside world are referred to as output neurons, the set of which constitutes the output layer.

We can now postulate a set of weights for the synapses between the input and hidden layers and between the hidden and output layers that will allow the network to emulate the behavior of the XOR function. The weights between the hidden-layer neurons and output-layer neurons are both +1. (There are two synapses that lie between the hidden and output layers.) These weights are such that when either both 0s or both 1s are applied, the hidden-layer neurons become 0. If a (1,0) or (0,1) input pattern is applied, one of the hidden-layer neurons becomes 1, which is enough to set the output-layer neuron to 1.

Let us examine this process in detail. Suppose we use the following activation function for our hidden-layer neurons:

$$f(x) = \begin{cases} 1 & \text{if } x > 0 \\ 0 & \text{if } x \leq 0 \end{cases}$$

where x is the sum of the activations of the input-layer neurons each multiplied by the synapse weight, as follows. (*Note:* This activation formula is slightly different from the one presented earlier since we are working with 1s and 0s instead of bipolar data, which uses 1s and -1s.)

$$x = \sum_{i=0}^{n} A_i w_i$$

where n is the number of incoming neurons, A is the vector of incoming neurons, and w is the vector of synaptic weights connecting the incoming neurons to the neurons we are examining.

Given this activation function, let's examine what happens when the inputs to the input neurons are 0 and 0. The sum of products of inputs and weights to the first hidden-layer neuron is 0 since each activation is 0. Thus, x for the function $f(x)$ is 0. So, based on $f(x)$, the output of the second neuron is 0. Since each hidden-layer neuron output is 0, the input to the activation function of the output neuron is zero, and so the output neuron is 0. Thus, for the input of (0,0), the output conforms to the XOR function.

If the input is (0,1), then the argument to the activation function of the first hidden-layer neuron is

$$(0 \times 1) + (1 \times -1) = -1$$

So the first hidden-layer neuron's activation becomes $f(-1) = 0$. The second hidden-layer neuron has the following total input to the activation function:

$$(0 \times -1) + (1 \times 1) = 1$$

So the second hidden-layer neuron's activation is $f(1) = 1$. The input to the output neuron is

$$(0 \times 1) + (1 \times 1) = 1$$

so its activation is $f(1)$, or 1. Thus, for the input of $(0,1)$ the result is also correct for the XOR function. Since the weight values for each layer of synapses are symmetric, the output for an input of $(1,0)$ is also 1.

If the input is $(1,1)$, the input to each hidden-layer neuron is 0, since the positive and negative incoming weights cancel each other. The activation of each hidden-layer neuron is therefore 0, and thus the output-layer neuron's input and activation are 0. For all possible inputs, the outputs conform to the expected behavior of the XOR function. Thus, given the correct weights, this network can emulate the exclusive-OR function. In general, any network with a hidden layer can learn nonlinear mappings.

2.4.1 Training Multilayer Networks

A problem remains. How can this multilayer network learn? How can we create the correct set of weights for an arbitrary nonlinear function? We cannot simply adjust the hidden layer of synapses using the simple error correction law presented. We need some way of adjusting the synaptic weights of layers away from the output neurons. This was actually the critique rendered by Minsky in *Perceptrons* [Minsky 69]: "Perhaps some powerful convergence theorem will be discovered, or some profound reason for the failure to produce an interesting 'learning theorem' for the multilayered machine will be found." Minsky was clearly skeptical, and this contributed to a subsequent long winter in neural network research. However, the solution to the problem is not really very complicated, and it is surprising to me that it was not discovered sooner: The weights for the synapses between the hidden and output layers are adjusted based on the output-layer neuron error multiplied by the hidden-layer neuron activation modulated by the learning rate. This is error correction as we saw previously, before introducing hidden layers.

The next stage is what allows us to compute the theoretical "hidden-layer neuron error": Take the error terms (deltas) of the output layer of neurons, and run them back over the synapses to each of the hidden-layer neurons (each hidden layer neuron accepts a weighted sum of the errors in the output layer). The "error" of each hidden layer neuron, then, is this sum multiplied by the activation of the hidden-layer neuron.

These "hidden-layer neuron errors" are used to calculate the changes for the weights between the input layer and the hidden layer in a manner similar to that used for computing the weight changes between the hidden and output layers. If we had more hidden layers, we could "backpropagate" these errors further still.

Actually, the standard backpropagation model and algorithm are a little more complicated. We present it in full as the first model in the next chapter. But the basic idea is fundamental to the training of all multilevel networks. Multilevel networks would certainly be of limited use if they could not be trained. And, of course, we have seen how limited two-layer networks are for a broad range of problems. Thus, this discovery was actually quite fundamental to the advancement of neural nets and can probably be credited with rescuing neural networks from obscurity.

3

NEURAL NET MODELS

In this chapter we present several neural net models in their classic form. This is not to say that the algorithms and topologies cannot be modified. (Indeed, one of the reasons for implementing all of this in C++ is to encourage such modification.) Emphasis is placed on those models with the most immediate practical value as tools to build applications, yet the intent is to present a reasonable cross section of the types of models available. For example, the perceptron (although historically significant and discussed earlier) has limited applicability for reasons that have been discussed, and it will not be presented here. Also, adaptive resonance theory is not presented, although other unsupervised learning models (notably counterpropagation) are.

As stated, we attempt to present a model in its classic form, but this should not be taken as a restriction on how techniques can be applied. For example, backpropagation of errors has applicability far beyond the "classic" simple backprop model we are about to present. Similarly, the "winner-take-all" first layer of the counterpropagation model can be used in many other situations.

The applications will be built in subsequent chapters with the aim of giving a sense of just how models might be modified (or even combined) to suit a given application. In fact, counterpropagation itself is a combination of two previously existing models (a Kohonen linear vector quantizer and a Grossberg outstar encoder). The C++ framework for all this code should make such explorations simple.

Also, we do not try to present a "cookbook" of every neural net ever conceived. This approach inevitably leads to much duplication in the techniques presented. Also, the resulting "catalog" would be fairly arbitrary. The idea is to provide a broad survey of the major neural net methods. With these in hand, along with the easily modified object-oriented framework of the code, it is relatively easy to create new models. (In fact, as suggested later in this chapter, you could combine counterpropagation and BAM Systems to produce counterpropagation networks that aren't plagued by capacity limitations.)

The three major models that will be presented (backprop, counterprop, and BAM System) provide a representative sample of the techniques available. Backpropagation demonstrates a multilayer network with supervised learning. In its canonical form, as presented here, it is certainly one of the most popular networks in applications. As emphasized repeatedly, its provision for training of hidden-layer weights overcame the major stumbling block to continued development of neural networks. This book therefore would not be complete without a detailed discussion of it. Counterpropagation demonstrates an unsupervised learning method, which for many applications is more practicable than backpropagation. It also (as just mentioned) incorporates two simpler important neural nets (Kohonen self-organizing nets and Grossberg encoders). The BAM System demonstrates a model whose building block is a simple two-layer network, and the technique of combining them to overcome capacity limitations should be readily applicable to other nets plagued by such limitations. It also demonstrates a binary discrete net, as opposed to the first two networks, which are presented as analog implementations.

These models have quite a bit in common. They will all be derived from the abstract neural network class. They will all have training, testing, and running methods. They will have methods for cycling through the full set of input-output pairs and methods for storing and retrieving weights to be used in the training process. They will have abstract encoding and recall methods, which will be made concrete based on the information in the next few sections. They will all be presented with input and output patterns whose size must be specified. They will all have learning rates, rates of weight decay (which may be zero), and tolerance levels to which they must be trained. These commonalities will be extracted from the abstract neural network discussed earlier. The subsequent discussion will be on the differences between the models.

For each model we will present the topology (the architecture of the neuron layers and synaptic connections for the model), the training (or encoding) algorithm, the recall algorithm, and a discussion of some of the fine points of the model. It is a reasonably straightforward transformation from these descriptions to a C++ implementation, so we will present the C++ classes here as well (but not the full code).

In describing the algorithm, we shall employ vector notation. Vectors are represented in **bold**, matrices are in **BOLD CAPS**. This should be easier to follow than a host of $\sum$s all over the place. The code itself will be written using vector and matrix arithmetic operators (using our vector and matrix classes, which we will provide with all the necessary overloaded operators). Using vector and matrix notation to describe the algorithms will provide a more direct translation to the code.

■ 3.1 BACKPROPAGATION

As we mentioned before, backpropagation of errors is a relatively generic concept. We will present here what might be considered a classic backprop model [Rumelhart, Hinton 86]. The backpropagation model is applicable to a wide class of problems. It is certainly the predominant supervised training algorithm. Supervised learning implies that we must have a set of "good" pattern associations to train with. In the classic backprop algorithm we present here, there are little or no self-organizing aspects. We must have a good set of teaching facts available, and a very good sense of the topology (in terms of input and output patterns and the number and size of hidden layers) appropriate to the problem, before we choose backprop to solve a problem.

The backprop model presented in Figure 3.1 has three layers of neurons: an input layer, a hidden layer, and an output layer. There are two layers of synaptic weights. There is a learning rate term, α, in the subsequent formulas, indicating how much of the weight change to effect on each pass. This is typically a number between 0 and 1. There is a momentum term, Θ, indicating how much a previous weight change should influence the current weight change. There is also a term indicating within what tolerance we can accept an output as "good."

3.1.1 Encoding

Assign random values between -1 and $+1$ to the weights between the input and hidden layers, the weights between the hidden and output layers, and the thresholds for the hidden-layer and output-layer neurons. Train the network by performing the following procedure for all pattern pairs.

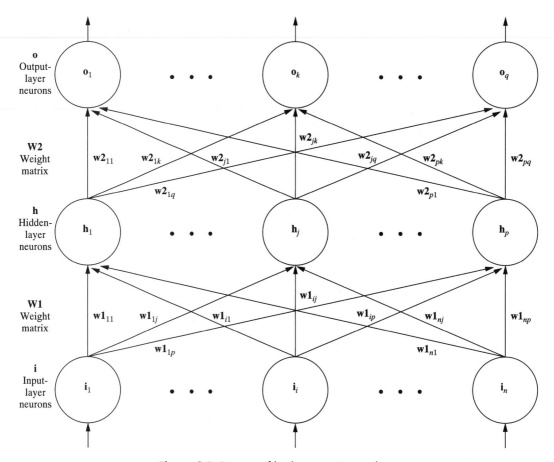

Figure 3.1 Diagram of backpropagation topology.

Forward Pass

1. Compute the hidden-layer neuron activations:

$$\mathbf{h} = F(\mathbf{iW1})$$

where **h** is the vector of hidden-layer neurons, **i** the vector of input-layer neurons, and **W1** the weight matrix between the input and hidden layers.

2. Compute the output-layer neuron activations:

$$\mathbf{o} = F(\mathbf{hW2})$$

where $\mathbf{o}$ represents the output layer, $\mathbf{h}$ the hidden layer, $\mathbf{W2}$ the matrix of synapses connecting the hidden and output layers, and $F()$ is a sigmoid activation function. We will use the logistic function

$$F(x) = \frac{1}{1 + e^{-x}}$$

Backward Pass

3. Compute the output-layer error (the difference between the target and the observed output):

$$\mathbf{d} = \mathbf{o}(1 - \mathbf{o})(\mathbf{o} - \mathbf{t})$$

where $\mathbf{d}$ is the vector of errors for each output neuron, $\mathbf{o}$ is the output-layer vector, and $\mathbf{t}$ is the target (correct) activation of the output layer.

4. Compute the hidden-layer error:

$$\mathbf{e} = \mathbf{h}(1 - \mathbf{h})\mathbf{W2d}$$

where $\mathbf{e}$ is the vector of errors for each hidden-layer neuron.

5. Adjust the weights for the second layer of synapses:

$$\mathbf{W2} = \mathbf{W2} + \Delta\mathbf{W2}$$

where $\Delta\mathbf{W2}$ is a matrix representing the change in matrix $\mathbf{W2}$. It is computed as follows:

$$\Delta\mathbf{W2}_t = \alpha\mathbf{hd} + \Theta\Delta\mathbf{W2}_{t-1}$$

where α is the learning rate and Θ is the momentum factor used to allow the previous weight change to influence the weight change in this time period, t. This does not mean that time is somehow incorporated into the model. It means only that a weight adjustment may depend to some degree on the previous weight adjustment made. This could also be called a *cycle*.

6. Adjust the weights for the first layer of synapses:

$$\mathbf{W1} = \mathbf{W1} + \mathbf{W1}_t$$

where

$$\mathbf{W1}_t = \alpha\mathbf{ie} + \Theta\Delta\mathbf{W1}_{t-1}$$

Repeat steps 1 to 6 on all pattern pairs until the output-layer error (vector **d**) is within the specified tolerance for each pattern and for each neuron.

3.1.2 Recall

Present the input pattern to the input layer of neurons of our backprop net:

1. Compute the hidden-layer activation:

$$\mathbf{h} = F(\mathbf{W1i})$$

2. Compute the output layer:

$$\mathbf{o} = F(\mathbf{W2h})$$

The vector **o** is our recalled pattern.

3.1.3 Discussion

3.1.3.1 Fine Points

We have left out some details in the preceeding encoding algorithm. These are mainly "options" in the implementation of the algorithm.

First of all, "thresholds" may be used for both the hidden and output layers. These thresholds are in effect biases on the computed activations. If we incorporate these terms, the formula for computing the hidden layer is:

$$\mathbf{h} = F(\mathbf{iW1} + \mathbf{thresh1})$$

The output-layer computation has a similar term added:

$$\mathbf{o} = F(\mathbf{W2h} + \mathbf{thresh2})$$

During training, the threshold vectors are adjusted based on the learning rate multiplied by the error vector for that layer of neurons:

$$\mathbf{thresh1} = \mathbf{thresh1} + \alpha\mathbf{d}$$

The recall process also has the threshold vector added to both the hidden- and output-layer computations. This approach may assist training somewhat, but threshold adjustment very often adds little to the process.

Also, the learning-rate term can be "cooled." α may start at some relatively high number (such as 0.5) and be reduced asymptotically to 0 (by halving the learning rate on each cycle through the patterns, for example). Again, this has not been found to be of great help, so it is left out of the implementation, but it could be easily added.

One fine point that has been included is the idea of "momentum." On each pass through the layers, the weight change of a matrix of synapses is influenced by the previous pass's weight change. The degree to which it is influenced is determined by the momentum term (typically a number from 0 to 1). Momentum can be extremely useful in helping networks to train faster, so it is implemented in our toolkit (it is settable in the definition file for a backprop net).

Also, the weight adjustments as we have discussed them are made as each pattern pair is encoded. However, weight adjustments can be made after the entire set of input pairs has been presented. This is referred to as "epoch-based" encoding. We keep track of the cumulative errors as we pass through the pattern pairs. At the end of a cycle (the "epoch"), we make weight adjustments based on teh accumulated error values. Our class library supports epoch-based encoding as an option.

3.1.3.2 *Hidden-Layer Size*

You may have noticed that we have not said anything about the size of each of the layers in the net. The sizes of the input and output layers will be determined by the application (the numbers of input factors and output factors). The hidden-layer size, though, is unspecified. A rule of thumb is for the size of this layer to be somewhere between the input-layer size (generally larger) and the output-layer size (possibly quite small).

However, the best size generally is determined by familiarity with the application. The hidden layer is the "generalizing layer." It takes input-layer neurons and tends to combine them into "meta"-groups. For example, in a character recognition application, the hidden layer may learn to group input-layer "pixel" neurons into features representing lines. Having some idea of the number of groupings of input neurons in an application may help us choose an appropriate number for the number of hidden-layer neurons. However, it is probably better to err on the side of too many hidden-layer neurons.

The backprop neural network in the toolkit can have the size of its input, hidden, and output layers (and other parameters, such as learning rate) set by a configuration file tied to the particular application. This should make it very easy to tune the size of the hidden layer to the particular application. (*Note*: All of the neural net models in the toolkit have their application-specific parameters set by a configuration file. Once the particular neural net model is chosen, no coding or recompilation is necessary to set the appropriate parameters for a particular application.)

3.1.3.3 *Strengths and Weaknesses*

The backpropagation network has the ability to learn any arbitrarily complex nonlinear mapping. This is due to the introduction of the hidden layer. It also has a capacity much greater than the dimensionality of its input and output layers. As we will see later, this is not true of all neural net models.

However, backpropagation can involve extremely long—potentially infinite—training times. If you have strong relationships between inputs and outputs and you are willing to accept results within a relatively broad tolerance, your training time may be reasonable. However, for applications where the relationships are subtle and where predictions must be relatively accurate, I have experienced training times of several *days* on a 33 MHz 386.

Hardware support for this algorithm (backprop chips, which are already appearing) should help matters quite a bit. Many components of the algorithm are highly parallel. The adjustments of the weight matrices and neuron activation vectors are all parallel procedures. The feed from one layer to the next for both training and recall must be performed sequentially (the hidden-layer neurons must be computed before the output-layer neurons can be). So most of backprop can be sped up with parallel hardware.

3.1.4 The Implementation

Following is the entire class definition for the backprop network. As stated earlier, we will not define all the methods here (the code for all the functions in the *bp* class), but the class definition will help to describe both the topology and the functionality of each model. Also remember that much of the substance of the class is simply inherited from the *net* class. Presented in the *bp* class are only the data and methods unique to backpropagation.

We can get an idea of the topology from the private section, where the data that is unique to backpropagation is kept. The *bp* class consists of two matrices representing the synaptic weights between the input and hidden layers and the weights between the hidden and output layers, and a vector representing the hidden layer. We do not need to explicitly represent the input and output layers, because they will be passed in as a vector argument to the *encode* method and passed back as the return from the *recall* method. There is also a number representing the momentum of the weight changes—how much a weight change in a previous time period affects the weight change in the current time period.

The implementation may perform *epoch-based updating* of weights, if this parameter is set in the definition file. Weights are then updated only once for each iteration through the complete set of input data. The total error is accumulated in the vectors **totd** and **tote**. This approach speeds training considerably. For some applications it may be appropriate to update weights after each individual input-output pair. In this case, remove the definition of EPOCH.

The functionality unique to backpropagation can be gleaned from the methods in the public part of the class. We must be able to construct the net from the parameters in a configuration file. This capability is given by the bp() constructor listed as a public method of the class. This constructor will actually call the constructor of the abstract parent class *net* to perform most of the work, as described earlier.

We need to be able to store pattern associations in the network, a capability provided by the *encode* method, which takes a vector pair as an argument. The *recall* method returns an output pattern vector based on a given input vector. Both of these methods are defined in the abstract neural network class, but they are pure virtual and must be overridden with defined methods to allow the *bp* class to be concrete.

Listing 3.1: Backprop Class Definition

```
// BP.HPP
// Header file for backprop implementation
// Copyright (c) 1990, Adam Blum
```

```
#include"vecmat.hpp"

class bp: public net {

private:
        int q; // size of the hidden layer
        matrix *W1,*W2; // weight matrices for the synapse layers
        matrix *dW1,*dW2; // used to compute change in weights
        vec *h,*o,*d,*e;  // vectors used to store:
                      // h - the hidden-layer neuron activations
                      // o - the output-layer result
                      // d - the target result
                      // e - the error vector
        vec *totd,*tote;  // used to accumulate total error
                          // for epoch-based updating
        vecpair *minvecs,*maxvecs; // used to "normalize" inputs
                                   // between min and max range
        float momentum; // how much weight change in previous
                        // time period affects weight change in
                        // current time period
int epoch; // indicates whether to perform "epoch-based" updating
         // of weights.

public:
        // constructor defined
        bp(char *s);                // constructs based on <name>.DEF file
~bp();                  // destructor
        // encode and recall methods must be
        // defined to override pure virtual methods and make this
        // class nonabstract
        int encode(vecpair& v); // store one pattern pair
        vec recall(vec& v);   // recall an output pattern given an input
};
```

3.1.5 The Test Program

The test program, TESTBP, constructs a backprop net from a file with the extension .DEF whose base name either is supplied as an argument to TESTBP or defaults to BP (BP.DEF) if no argument is supplied. The .DEF file contains the following parameters:

> INPUTS: The size of the input layer
> HIDDEN: The size of the hidden layer
> OUTPUTS: The size of the output layer
> RATE: The learning rate of the weight matrices
> MOMENTUM: The momentum of the weight changes
> TOLERANCE: The tolerance within which we will accept an output as valid

The file format is a set of keyword-value pairs in any order for all the parameters we wish to define. An example is:

> INPUTS 318
> OUTPUTS 30
> HIDDEN 64
> RATE 0.5
> MOMENTUM 0.2
> TOLERANCE 0.1

Note that this is implemented simply by invoking the constructor for the *bp* class and subsequently invoking the constructor for the *net* class to read in the parameters relevant to the generic network class (all but HIDDEN and MOMENTUM, so the *bp* class constructor only has to look for these two parameters).

TESTBP will train on a fact file (with a .FCT extension) containing all the input-output pattern pairs that we want to train with. The fact file's first line is a vector of the minimums for the input factors, followed by a comma, followed by the minimums for all the output factors. The second line contains the maximums for the input and output factors. The third line is a comment or header line, which begins with a : and generally has the name of each input and output factor in the proper column to label the data. All subsequent lines contain the actual facts (the input-output pairs, separated by commas).

The minimums and maximums are used to "normalize" the values of the inputs and outputs. Each piece of data in the fact file is converted to a number between 0 and 1 based on the range specified by the minimum and maximum allowed for that factor. Any values above or below the specified minimum and maximum (which could easily happen as we get new data) will simply be converted to 0 or 1, respectively.

Training is stopped when the network is able to predict all output factors of all facts within the specified tolerance. The network is then considered to be "trained." You can also suspend training by pressing a key during the training process. In either case, the network's weights are then stored in a weights file (with a .WTS extension). If training was suspended, a subsequent request for training will automatically resume training from the stored weights.

When invoked with a "-T" option, TESTBP will test a trained network on the facts stored in the test file (with a .TST extension). The test file has the same format of minimum line, maximum line, header, and facts. TESTBP can be run with the "-R" option. It needs a file of input patterns (with a .IN extension) in the same format of minimum line, maximum line, header, and facts, and it will create a file of outputs (with a .OUT extension) corresponding to these inputs.

These file extension naming conventions are used throughout the neural network toolkit. All the neural net implementations require basically the same set of files: files for definition (.DEF files), training data (.FCT files), test data (.IN files), and test results (.OUT files). Users of California Scientific Software's Brainmaker may recognize these conventions and should be able to immediately remember what file extension means what. Be careful, however, as the file structures themselves are not identical. McClelland and Rumelhart in *Explorations in Parallel Distributed Processing* [Rumelhart 89] use another set of file extension conventions for a similar set of uses. We could just as easily have used theirs or invented a new set of extensions.

3.1.6 A Note about Speed and Optimization

As mentioned, backpropagation is slow. This problem can be alleviated in several ways. First, we can make the C++ code as efficient as possible. Toward this end, several compromises have been made in terms of immediate understandability of the code in order to combine functions for speed, although we don't want to get too carried away in this regard. Remember, we are trying to use the code as a rather high-level description of what is going on—a sort of "working pseudocode." In the backprop *encode* method this goal has to some extent been compromised, because this is certainly where the speed bottleneck in training lies. However, for those seriously interested in improving training speed, further improvements could certainly be made by "merging" functions called by *encode*. This involves coding the functions called by *encode* inline, eliminating the overhead of a function call (a very expensive operation on the 80x86 architecture).

The next step beyond merging functions (improving the code at the C/C++ level) is, of course, optimizing expensive operations with assembly. A major candidate for this optimization is the matrix-vector multiplication performed during each pass through a layer of weights (in either a forward or backward direction). A second candidate is matrix addition (for performing weight layer updates). Eberhart and Dobbins do an admirable job of presenting assembly code (80x86 assembler) for these operations in their book *Neural Network PC Tools* [Eberhart 90]. We shall not try to replicate their work, as it is not appropriate to our focus on reusable general tools. Only those disappointed with the performance of their backpropagation applications, *and constrained for some reason to a single-processor PC environment,* should feel compelled to resort to this approach.

Of course, since the most expensive operations are floating-point operations, we can also get quite an improvement from using math coprocessors. The Intel 80x87 family (as appropriate for your CPU) is certainly an option. The 80486 even includes such a coprocessor (an 80387) built into the chip. Perhaps more interesting is the Weitek chip. Weitek provides numeric coprocessors for the

Intel family of CPUs that are often several times faster than the equivalent Intel coprocessor. Make sure that your motherboard has a socket for the Weitek chip (it is not the same as the 80x87 socket) before ordering the product. If the compiler directly supports Weitek (by taking advantage of Weitek's pipelining capabilities, for example), you can achieve even greater speedups. Zortech and Borland C++ do not directly support Weitek, but those systems using a C++ preprocessor could use Metaware High-C 386 as the back end of their C++ compiler. Metaware does support explicit Weitek optimizations.

Another means of optimization is to specify certain variables as "register" variables. However, in the 80x86 architecture (PCs) we only have two registers available to us. For most of the code here, it is a relatively simple matter to determine what two variables should be registers—generally, these are the indexes to our loops through vectors and matrices. In fact, it is such a simple choice that most PC compilers (and certainly the ones we use here) pick up the optimization every time. Most of the methods of the classes in the toolkit are very small functions. Rarely does the compiler optimizer have to choose among separate inner FOR loops in a function to assign a register. Thus, for the majority of the toolkit, registers are not assigned manually. In other architectures, (such as the MIPS chip that powers the DECstation 5000 I often use for compute-intensive problems), there are many registers to choose from. On these platforms, it is definitely worth the effort for the programmer to expend some effort assigning registers by hand. Some judgments can be made effectively only with knowledge of, for example, run-time control flow and become important after the first few obvious register assignments are made.

The best solution is simply to move to parallel hardware. Hand-optimizing HLL code or hand-coding assembly routines provides speedups in percentages. Moving to parallel hardware provides speedups in orders of magnitude. And only parallel hardware fully exploits the advantages of the neural network approach.

Figure 3.2 is a diagram of the class hierarchy for the backpropagation network. See Appendix I for full listings of the backpropagation implementation.

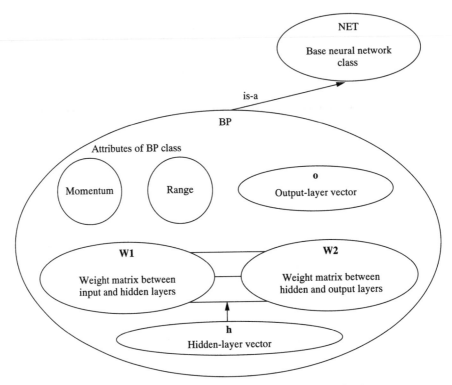

Note: Objects within BP used only for intermediate computations are not depicted.

Figure 3.2 Class hierarchy for backpropagation.

■ 3.2 COUNTERPROPAGATION

Another multiple-layer network, invented by Robert Hecht-Nielsen, is the counterpropagation network (CPN) [Hecht-Nielsen 87]. Counterpropagation networks train much faster than backprop nets. They also have the capability to generalize. This allows them to handle well data that is erroneous or that has not been seen before.

As stated previously, counterpropagation is actually a combination of two other models, the Kohonen linear vector quantizer and the Grossberg outstar encoder. The study of this model will also highlight the advantages of Kohonen self-organizing networks (of which the linear vector quantizer is an example) and Grossberg outstar encoders. The Kohonen layer demonstrates the generalization and "lookup table" capabilities of self-organizing networks. The Grossberg layer demonstrates the outstar's ability to act as a minimal pattern encoder. However, the CPN has capabilities beyond either of these individual networks.

3.2.1 Topology

Counterpropagation networks are three-layer (input pattern, hidden layer, and output pattern) structures with two layers of connectivity (synapses). The synapses between the input layer and the hidden layer act as a winner-take-all vector quantizer of input patterns. For each input pattern, the hidden-layer neuron whose vector of synapses to the input layer is most similar to the input pattern is chosen as the winning neuron, effectively "categorizing" the input pattern. The second layer of synapses (the Grossberg outstar encoder) has its weights adjusted on each pattern association based upon the activation of the winning hidden-layer neuron and the output vector. The CPN network topology is illustrated in Figure 3.3.

3.2.2 Encoding

The weights between the input and hidden layers are initialized to random values. An input pattern is presented to the CPN, and the hidden-layer neuron whose weight vector is closest to this input pattern is chosen. (The vector distance function is simply the sum of squared differences between individual elements.) The chosen weight vector in the Kohonen layer is then adjusted

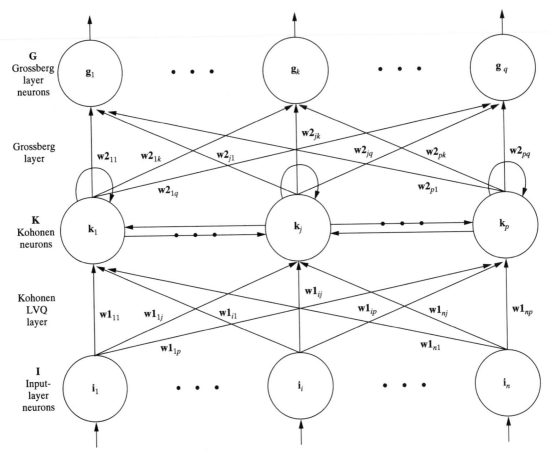

Figure 3.3 Diagram of counterpropagation network topology.

based on the difference between the weight vector and the input vector, tempered by the learning rate at time t (in our implementation we get the learning rate for a particular time by just decaying the learning rate over time).

The weights between the winning neuron in the hidden layer and each neuron of the output layer are then adjusted by the production of the winning neuron's activation and each output neuron activation, modified by a learning rate constant.

3.2.3 Recall

For recall, a pattern is presented to the input layer, fed through the first layer of weights, to come up with a vector of activations for the hidden layer of neurons. Whichever activation is strongest is chosen as the winning neuron, and the corresponding vector of weights to the output layer is chosen as the output pattern.

3.2.4 Discussion

3.2.4.1 Enhancements

Counterpropagation's unsupervised learning capability is one of its greatest strengths. However, it is possible to create a supervised learning version with the same CPN topology described here. It is also possible to have "multiple winners"; more than one neuron may be activated in the hidden layer. Provision for multiple-winner CPN is made in the code.

3.2.4.2 Disadvantages

One big weakness of the CPN is the need to have an individual hidden-layer neuron for each output pattern we want learned. In other words, the capacity is n patterns, where n is the number of hidden-layer neurons. An inventive solution to the neural network capacity problem (which exists in most neural net models) is explored in the next section, on BAM Systems. It is likely that the same approach used for BAM Systems (creating a new matrix of connectivity when one is saturated) could prove effective in extending the usefulness of CPNs.

3.2.5 The Implementation

3.2.5.1 *The Code*

The Layer Class

Two basic classes are supplied in the CPN implementation: the layer class, and the CPN class. The layer class is derived from the class matrix (remember, the vector and matrix classes are our building blocks) and, beyond being just a matrix, has a learn rate and a decay term. (*Layer* refers to a layer of synapses, not a layer of neurons, although in the text description the fields of neurons are called "layers." I apologize for the confusion, which runs through much of the literature in the field.) Following the *bp* definition is a definition for the layer class.

Thus, there are two "layers" (of synapses) in our CPN—one for the Kohonen vector quantizer and one for the Grossberg outstar encoder. The layer class will be used quite often in our development of other neural nets. Regardless of where this class is used, if it represents the weights between two fields of neurons, it is likely to have the same data representation. That is, it is likely to be a matrix, with an associated value representing the decay of those weights over time and another value representing the learning rate due to any one *encode* operation. The operations available for a layer will generally be a constructor (to make a layer), a destructor (to get rid of it), and a function to change weights. For the CPN, we needed to provide separate weight-changing functions for Kohonen and Grossberg layers. We might prefer to do this at the CPN class level, but we need access to the private data of the layer class to change these weights.

The layer class definition is:

```
class layer: public matrix {
        double learnrate;
        double decay;
public:
        void chgwts_koh(int c,vec& input);
        void chgwts_gross(int r,double activation,vec& output);
```

```
layer(int n,int p,double randlimit,double r,double d):
matrix(n,p,randlimit){learnrate=r;decay=d;}
~layer(){};
};
```

The CPN Class

The CPN class consists of pointers to the Kohonen and Grossberg layers and indicators (n, p, q) of the dimensionality of the CPN. The Kohonen layer is n by p; the Grossberg layer is p by q. Notice that we only have a data representation for the weight matrices (layers). We don't need to store any of the neuron layers; these are implied. The input layer of neurons (n neurons long) is supplied to the CPN on *encode* or *recall*. The output layer of neurons (q neurons long) is returned on *recall*, and supplied on *encode*. The hidden layer of neurons is computed on the fly and does not need to be stored.

The "noise" term shown in the private section of the class allows us to train on noisy data without manually putting such data into the training set. As each pattern association is read in from the .FCT file, each number in the pattern is corrupted with a probability given by the noise term. If the noise term is 0.1, the data is subjected to 10 percent noise. Remember, the first layer of the CPN, the Kohonen LVQ, excels at generalization. Training is actually improved with data that is noisy to some extent.

Also, a count of wins for each hidden-layer neuron is kept (int *wins in the class definition). This is because, for many applications, the designation of "winning neuron" can cluster to the same neuron (or neurons). We thus use the count of neuron wins to inhibit the same neuron from winning again. The scaling term controls the level of this inhibition. Another enhancement to the standard CPN is the multiwinner CPN, mentioned earlier. The number of winners is determined by the network definition file and is stored as the *winners* term of the network.

The basic capabilities required of the CPN are identical to what we need from the backpropagation network. Methods are provided to *encode* an input-output pattern pair and to *recall* an output pattern given an input pattern vector. You can *train* a CPN from a file of input-output pattern pairs or facts (this file has a .FCT extension), or you can *run* a CPN from a file of input patterns (from a .IN file) and write the output patterns out (to a .OUT file). The constructor for the CPN reads the CPN's parameters from a .DEF file.

The CPN layer class definition is:

```
class cpn: public net {
        int n,p;
        layer *koh;
        layer *gross;
        double noise;
        double range;

int *wins; // keep track of wins for each Kohonen neuron
        double scaling;
        int winners;

public:
        int iters;
        cpn(char *s);
        ~cpn(){};
        void encode(const vecpair& AC);
        vec recall(vec& A);
        void train();
        void run();
}; // network layer class
```

Figure 3.4 shows the class hierarchy for the counterpropogation network.

3.2.5.2 The Test Program

The test program, TESTCPN, constructs a CPN from a file with the extension .DEF whose base name either is supplied as an argument to TESTCPN or defaults to CPN (CPN.DEF) if no argument is supplied. The .DEF file contains the following parameters:

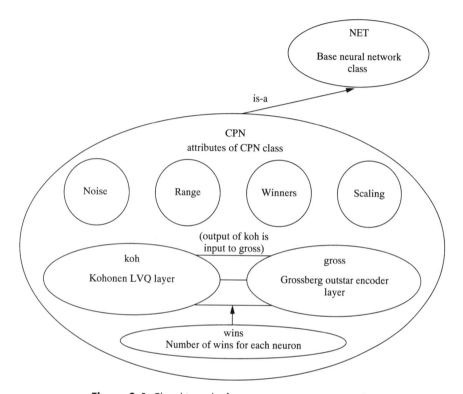

Figure 3.4 Class hierarchy for counterpropagation network.

The size of the input layer

The size of the hidden layer

The size of the output layer

The learning rate of the Kohonen linear vector quantizer (we will actually decay this rate to lower values, however)

The learning rate of the Grossberg layer

The decay rate of the Grossberg layer

The value to use as the high end of the range to randomize the values of the initial weights in the Kohonen layer

The number of times to iterate through our set of training facts to train the CPN

TESTCPN will train on a fact file (with a .FCT extension) containing all the input-output pattern pairs we want to train with. If we run our CPN, it will run on a test file of just input patterns (with a .IN extension) and create a file of output corresponding to these inputs (with a .OUT extension).

In a subsequent chapter, we will present an application of this generalized mechanism in which pixellated images of digits are mapped to the digits themselves. In this application the definition (.DEF) file specifies 64 neurons for input (an 8×8 image) and 10 neurons for output (a vector with one nonzero element indicating the digit). The learning rate is generally set at 0.2 for both the Kohonen and Grossberg layers but may be varied as we will see later. The high end of the range over which to randomize the initial weight values is set to 1. The number of neurons in the hidden layer is set to 24, but this is arbitrary, and part of our experiment is to vary this parameter. We will describe the results of running the CPN on this application later.

■ 3.3 BIDIRECTIONAL ASSOCIATIVE MEMORIES AND BAM SYSTEMS

Content addressability was a consistent goal of early neural network pioneers. Indeed, it is a quest that has been pursued by computer scientists in general for decades. However, the goal has proved highly elusive. Search time has always depended on the amount of data stored, although much research has gone into reducing the slope of this curve. Real-time pattern recognition (as applied to any of a number of fields, including speech recognition, radar signature identification, and part classification) is still far from realization. However, one particular neural network construct, BAM (or bidirectional associative memory) holds some promise toward the solution of this problem. We will first describe the BAM concept. We will then show how a relatively recent construct, the BAM System, may make it immediately feasible for real problems.

3.3.1 BAMs

3.3.1.1 Topology

As developed by Bart Kosko, bidirectional associative memories are a neural network–based attempt at content-addressable memories [Kosko 88]. Based on two-layer feedback neural networks, they attempt to encode m pattern pairs $(\mathbf{A}_i, \mathbf{B}_i)$, where, $\mathbf{A}_i \in \{-1, +1\}^n$ and $\mathbf{B}_i \in \{-1, +1\}^p$, in an $n \times p$ matrix $\mathbf{M}$. They are globally stable and provide instant recall of either of the two pattern-pair elements. However, they face some limitations. For large pattern lengths n, storage requirements increase $O(n^2)$. That is, the amount of memory required for the BAM grows at least as fast as the square of the pattern length. More importantly, storage capacity is only, on average, $m < \min(n, p)$. Thus, for moderate pattern lengths, the capacity of the matrix $\mathbf{M}$ becomes a problem, although recent research promises some help in resolving this problem. Figure 3.5 illustrates the BAM topology.

3.3.1.2 Encoding

BAM encoding is accomplished by simply summing the correlation matrices of each of the pattern pairs. That is, the matrix that encodes the first m pattern pairs, $\mathbf{M}$, is simply:

$$\mathbf{M} = \sum_{i=1}^{m} \mathbf{A}_i^T \mathbf{B}_i$$

Thus, to encode a pattern pair, simply produce its correlation matrix, $\mathbf{A}_i^T \mathbf{B}_i$, and add the values to the current matrix $\mathbf{M}$. For discrete implementations, it happens that the matrix arithmetic works out better if 0s and 1s are encoded as -1s and $+1$s. So the first step in the process is to convert any $\{0, 1\}$ string to $\{-1, +1\}$.

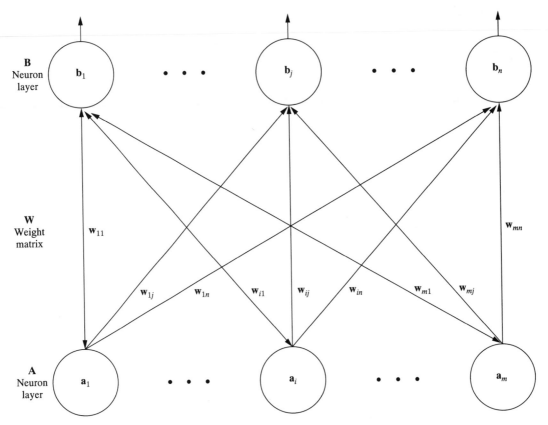

Figure 3.5 Diagram of BAM system topology.

Following is an example of this whole process. If we are trying to encode

$$\mathbf{A}_1 = (101010) \qquad \mathbf{B}_1 = (1100)$$
$$\mathbf{A}_2 = (111000) \qquad \mathbf{B}_2 = (1010)$$

we first convert to $\{-1, +1\}$. Then

$$\mathbf{X}_1 = (1 \quad -1 \quad 1 \quad -1 \quad 1 \quad -1) \qquad \mathbf{Y}_1 = (1 \quad 1 \quad -1 \quad -1)$$
$$\mathbf{X}_2 = (1 \quad 1 \quad 1 \quad -1 \quad -1 \quad -1) \qquad \mathbf{Y}_2 = (1 \quad -1 \quad 1 \quad -1)$$

and

$$\mathbf{X}_1^T \mathbf{Y}_1 = \begin{array}{rrrr} 1 & 1 & -1 & -1 \\ -1 & -1 & 1 & 1 \\ 1 & 1 & -1 & -1 \\ -1 & -1 & 1 & 1 \\ 1 & 1 & -1 & -1 \\ -1 & -1 & 1 & 1 \end{array}$$

$$\mathbf{X}_2^T \mathbf{Y}_2 = \begin{array}{rrrr} 1 & -1 & 1 & -1 \\ 1 & -1 & 1 & -1 \\ 1 & -1 & 1 & -1 \\ -1 & 1 & -1 & 1 \\ -1 & 1 & -1 & 1 \\ -1 & 1 & -1 & 1 \end{array}$$

$$\mathbf{M} = \begin{array}{rrrr} 2 & 0 & 0 & -2 \\ 0 & -2 & 2 & 0 \\ 2 & 0 & 0 & -2 \\ -2 & 0 & 0 & 2 \\ 0 & 2 & -2 & 0 \\ -2 & 0 & 0 & 2 \end{array}$$

Note that we can erase association $(\mathbf{A}_i, \mathbf{B}_i)$ from $\mathbf{M}$ by adding $-\mathbf{X}_i^T \mathbf{Y}_i$ to $\mathbf{M}$. But if we are using a $\{-1, +1\}$ representation, this is the same as adding $(\mathbf{A}_i, \mathbf{B}_i\mathbf{C})$ or $(\mathbf{A}_i\mathbf{C}, \mathbf{B}_i)$ to $\mathbf{M}$ (where $\mathbf{C}$ represents the pattern's complement). This fact will become important in our implementation of the BAM System.

3.3.1.3 *Recall*

After we have trained our BAM with the m pattern pairs $(\mathbf{A}_i, \mathbf{B}_i)$, we wish it to recall pattern $\mathbf{B}_i$ every time $\mathbf{A}_i$ is presented to the matrix (and, conversely, recall $\mathbf{A}_i$ every time $\mathbf{B}_i$ is presented to the matrix). It turns out that BAMs also have the property that $\mathbf{B}_i$ will be recalled every time something close to $\mathbf{A}_i$ is presented. The following steps outline the decoding process involved in this.

Each neuron $\mathbf{B}_j$ in field $\mathbf{F}_b$ ($\mathbf{F}_a$ and $\mathbf{F}_b$ will be used to refer to the two pattern fields $\mathbf{A}$ and $\mathbf{B}$) receives a gated input of all the neurons in $\mathbf{F}_a$ with a nonlinear threshold function applied. In our discrete example, a typical function might be

$$f(x, y) = \begin{cases} 1 & \text{if } x > 0 \\ y & \text{if } x = 0 \\ 0 & \text{if } x < 0 \end{cases}$$

We now have a pattern $\mathbf{B}_1$. However, we aren't done yet. The output from pattern $\mathbf{B}$ is then fed back through the transpose of matrix $\mathbf{M}$ to produce pattern $\mathbf{A}_1$. That is, each neuron $\mathbf{A}_i$ in $\mathbf{A}$ receives gated input from each neuron $\mathbf{B}_j$ in $\mathbf{B}$ and applies the same threshold function to it. $\mathbf{A}_1$ is then sent back through the matrix again to produce $\mathbf{B}_2$. And on this goes.

$$\mathbf{A} \rightarrow F(\mathbf{AM}) \rightarrow \mathbf{B}_1$$
$$\mathbf{A}_1 \leftarrow F(\mathbf{B}_1\mathbf{M}^T) \leftarrow \mathbf{B}_1$$
$$\mathbf{A}_1 \rightarrow F(\mathbf{A}_1\mathbf{M}) \rightarrow \mathbf{B}_2$$
$$\vdots$$
$$\mathbf{A}_i \rightarrow F(\mathbf{A}_i) \rightarrow \mathbf{B}_i$$
$$\mathbf{A}_i \rightarrow F(\mathbf{B}_i\mathbf{M}) \rightarrow \mathbf{B}_i$$

But it won't go on forever. As shown, eventually the fields will "resonate" to steady patterns. This property of BAMs is called *global stability*. Lyapunov energy functions allow us to prove that BAMs are globally stable.

3.3.1.4 Discussion

Energy Functions and Stability

Lyapunov showed that any function expressed in terms of the system parameters that is zero at the origin and has nonincreasing changes is globally stable. An energy function for the BAM can be expressed as

$$E(\mathbf{A}, \mathbf{B}) = -\mathbf{AWB}^T$$

This function is obviously zero at the origin (that is, when $\mathbf{A}$ and $\mathbf{B}$ are zero). We just need to show that it has nonincreasing changes.

$$\Delta E_{\mathbf{A}}(\mathbf{A}, \mathbf{B}) = -\Delta \mathbf{AWB}^T$$

and, by the definition of our function f, each $\mathbf{A}_i$ in $\mathbf{A}$ will be positive only if $\mathbf{W}_i\mathbf{B}$ is positive. If $\mathbf{A}_i$ is negative, $\mathbf{W}_i\mathbf{B}$ must also be negative. Thus, the change in energy will always be negative or zero. The system is therefore globally stable.

Adaptive BAM

As we have just described it, the connection matrix $\mathbf{M}$ is simply the sum of the correlation matrices of the patterns presented to it. We can use more sophisticated equations to allow faster convergence or more accurate recall.

As long as such equations can also be shown to converge, this should be no problem.

The simplest learnings law is called Hebb's law:

$$\Delta \mathbf{m}_{ij} = -\mathbf{m}_{ij} + f_i(x_i) \times f_j(y_j)$$

where m_{ij} is the connection weight between the neuron x_i and neuron y_j, and f_i and f_j are the threshold activation functions for x and y, respectively.

Several other laws could be used, such as competitive learning or differential Hebb, and there is much research on which of these is most effective. In our implementation we will present a simple nonadaptive BAM. However, it is easily extensible to the learning function of choice.

Problems

BAM is faced with two problems. The amount of storage taken up varies by $O(n^2)$, where n is the pattern length. (*Note*: actually, it will vary $O(np)$, where n is pattern length of **A** and p is pattern length of **B**.) But the major problem with BAM is capacity. Reliable retrieval of associations begins to degrade when the number of patterns stored, m, is greater than the minimum of the two pattern dimensions. In other words, for reliable results the matrix capacity is

$$\mathbf{m} < \min(n, \ p)$$

For large pattern lengths this is not as much of a problem, but many applications have inherently moderate pattern lengths. Intuitively, it is obvious that if a BAM can only store up to the minimum of its pattern lengths, it will be useless for real-world applications.

3.3.2 BAM Systems

3.3.2.1 Topology

In 1989 Patrick Simpson introduced the concept of a "BAM System" [Simpson 90]. This is a rather uninformative name for a system that allows for multiple matrices when one matrix's capacity is saturated. Perhaps a better name would be "multimatrix BAM" or, since each matrix is just a representation of the connectivity between the two patterns, "multiconnective BAM." Whatever you choose to call it, it is an inventive way to overcome the severe problem of matrix capacity. This capacity problem is not limited to just the BAM (remember, we had the same problem with CPN), so this work is of fundamental importance.

3.3.2.2 Encoding

The BAM System operates as follows: Pattern pairs are encoded one by one in a single BAM matrix, M_1. After each pattern pair is encoded, the matrix must be tested to ensure that each pattern pair stored in it can be recalled. If a pattern pair cannot be recalled, the current pair is removed from the matrix. We then attempt to store the pair in another connection matrix. We continue to try to store it in other matrices, M_i, until a matrix is found such that all pattern pairs in that matrix can be recalled successfully. The pattern association is then permanently stored in this matrix.

3.3.2.3 Recall

Decoding, that is, presenting half of a pattern and recalling the other half of the pair, is a bit more complicated. Since we now have several matrices storing pattern associations, we don't know which one to look in to recall the pattern pair. To choose a pair out of the recalled pattern pairs from each matrix, we use the following criterion. We determine all the returned pattern pairs (X_i, Y_i) that have the same energy as the pair (A, Y_i) (where A is the presented pattern). We choose that pattern pair whose energy is closest to the matrix's orthogonal BAM energy. (*Note*: Orthogonal BAM energy is the energy a matrix would have if all its stored patterns were orthogonal, which turns out to be equal to the negative of the product of the pattern lengths, $E* = -np$. Energy of a pattern pair can be calculated in the same way as in our previous discussions, $E = -\mathbf{X}\mathbf{M}\mathbf{Y}^T$ where $\mathbf{X}$ and $\mathbf{Y}$ are the two patterns.)

3.3.2.4 Discussion

There are some problems with the BAM System. So that we may check that the patterns were stored reliably in each matrix (without corrupting the other patterns already in the matrix), the patterns need to be stored separately. Also, the need to compute the "best" recall from each of the BAM matrices could be computationally prohibitive. However, parallel hardware (which a BAM presumably would be running on anyway) could possibly ease this burden.

What Can You Do with It?

The uses of the BAM System are limited only by your imagination. Obvious uses include optical character recognition (the pixel patterns scanned in would be associated with the actual letters), voice recognition (the acoustic pattern would be associated with the actual word), and a super spell checker (word patterns would be associated with phonemestring patterns). The BAM System can be used for just about any application where you have a large number of "associations" that you would like be able to recall nearly instantaneously, and where some tolerance for error would be useful.

As an example of current uses, at the latest (January 1990) International Joint Conference on Neural Networks, a successful application of BAM for radar signature classification was presented. However, it was not a BAM System, and the implementors had to resort to various other tricks to get around capacity limitations. Several other associative memory applications have appeared, but none of them were associative memory systems, and eventually they all would presumably run into the capacity roadblock for large data sets. Associative memories and BAMs have begun to be implemented in VLSI, but again the capacity will prove to be a limitation for practical work. BAM Systems should have a radical effect on the usefulness of these chips.

Conclusions

Bidirectional associative memories appear to provide the content-addressable memory long sought after by computer scientists. They provide instant recall of pattern association, tolerance for error and fuzziness in the provided pattern, and global stability. However, they are subject to some limitations. The number of pattern pairs that a simple BAM matrix can encode is limited by the smaller of its two dimensions. Some applications have inherently small pattern length, and for these problems matrix capacity will prove to be a severe handicap. However, a new construct, the BAM System, appears to overcome this problem, making associative memory a reality.

3.3.2.5   *The Implementation*

The Classes

Once we have the vector, matrix, and vector pair classes, implementing the BAM is fairly simple. The BAM is essentially just a matrix, so we use the C++ inheritance mechanism to inherit the matrix and all its functions. The matrix's data structures are protected instead of private so that the derived BAM matrix class can use matrix's data structures. We now just add a *vecpair* pointer for the pattern pair list, and the BAM matrix functions. These consist mainly of the *encode* and *recall* functions central to the BAM. *Encode* simply takes the vector pair corresponding to the association and adds it (with matrix add) to the current BAM. *Recall* feeds the presented pattern through the matrix (with dot-products and applying a threshold function, as discussed previously) to return another vector. We keep feeding the vectors back and forth until they stabilize to a consistent pattern association. There are also some auxiliary functions for checking the integrity of the BAM, returning its energy for a particular association (as discussed earlier), and for "uncoding," or removing an association from the BAM. Notice that we do not inherit the network class at this level. We are not envisioning performing training on individual BAMs. Therefore, we wait until we have evolved the BAM System before making the system into a child of our neural network class.

```
class bam_matrix: public matrix {
        private:
                int K; // number of patterns stored in matrix
                vecpair *C; // actual pattern pairs stored
                int feedthru(const vec&A, vec& B);
                int sigmoid(int n); // sigmoid threshold function
        public:
                bam_matrix(int n=ROWS, int p=COLS);
                ~bam_matrix();
                void encode(const vecpair& AB); // self-ref version
                // uncode only necessary for BAM system
                void uncode(const vecpair& AB); // self-ref version
                vecpair recall(const vec& A);
                int check();
                int check(const vecpair& AB);
                // Lyapunov energy function: E=-AWBtranspose
                int energy(const matrix& m1); // Lyapunov energy function
}; // BAM matrix
```

The BAM System class simply consists of an array of pointers to BAM matrices. Each time a BAM matrix is saturated, a new matrix is created and the new pattern association stored in it. The major functions are, again, *encode* and *recall*. *Encode* attempts to store the pattern association in each of the BAM matrices until it succeeds. If it runs out of matrices, it will create a new ones. *Recall* performs a BAM matrix recall operation on each of the matrices. Whichever returned association is closest to the presented pattern and has the lowest energy relative to its matrix (as discussed before) is then returned as the "correct" pattern association. Another function is provided to "train" the BAM System from a specified file of pattern associations. The patterns happen to be represented as 01 strings, but they could be easily changed to whatever representation (such as floating-point numbers or character strings) suits the specific application.

```
class bam_system: public net {
        bam_matrix *W[MAXMATS];
        int M; // number of matrices
    public:
        bam_system(int M=1);
        ~bam_system();
        void encode(const vecpair& AB);
        vecpair& recall(const vec& A);
        // train equiv. to Simpson's encode of all pairs
        friend ostream& operator<<(ostream& s,bam_system& b);
}; // BAM system class
```

Figure 3.6 presents the class hierarchy for BAM Systems.

■ 3.4 HOPFIELD NETS

The Hopfield net is a single-layer auto-associative pattern storage mechanism [Hopfield 85]. The information retrieval application will use a straightforward manifestation of this model. The presentation here describes our information storage mechanism almost exactly. Our traveling salesman application, however, gets a bit more complicated than the topology shown in Figure 3.7.

3.4.1 Encoding

For discrete Hopfield nets, encoding is accomplished simply by adding the product of the activations of the neurons at both ends of the synapse to the weight stored in the synapse. That is,

$$\mathbf{W} = \sum \mathbf{A}_k^T \mathbf{A}_k$$

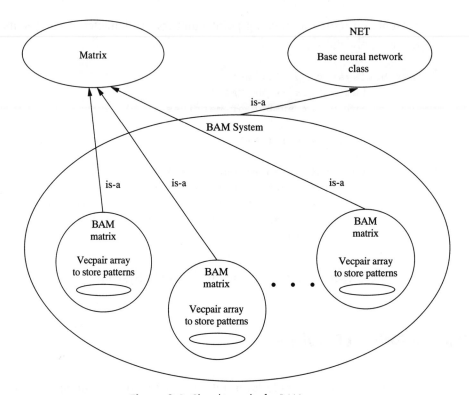

Figure 3.6 Class hierarchy for BAM systems.

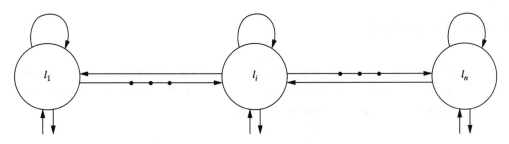

Figure 3.7 Diagram of Hopfield network topology.

where $\mathbf{W}$ represents the matrix of synapses and $\mathbf{A}_k$ represents the kth pattern to be stored.

For continuous Hopfield nets, the encoding formula is more flexible (and powerful). Encoding can be viewed as the process of formulating a set of conduction strengths, each modulated by a resistance:

$$w_{ij} = f(a_j)/R_{ij}$$

where w_{ij} is the conductance between the ith and jth neurons, a_j is the activity of the jth neuron, $f(a_j)$ is a formula based on the activity of the jth neuron, and R_{ij} is the resistance between the ith and jth neurons. There is no set formula for the modulation of a_j's activity ($f(a_j)$) or for determining appropriate values for R_{ij}. However, this is a powerful freedom that we will use later in designing a weight adjustment formula that will lead to optimal solutions of the traveling salesman problem.

In vector notation, the formula is

$$\mathbf{W}_i = f(\mathbf{A})/\mathbf{R}_i$$

3.4.2 Recall

Recall is performed simply by presenting a pattern to the neurons of the Hopfield net and letting it cascade back and forth through the synapses until it stabilizes to a steady retrieved pattern. A nonlinear threshold function is used to control the activation of the neurons. In the information retrieval application, we use a discrete Hopfield net (also known as a "discrete autocorrelator"), so this function is simply the step function.

$$f(x) = \begin{cases} 1 & \text{if } x > 0 \\ -1 & \text{if } x < 0 \\ \text{unchanged} & \text{if } x = 0 \end{cases}$$

For continuous Hopfield, the formula is, again, more complicated but more powerful and begins to reveal some advantages over a more simple matrix associative memory. In vector notation (since this is how it will be coded),

$$\mathbf{A}_{t+1} = S(\mathbf{A}_t)\mathbf{W} - \mathbf{A}_t/\mathbf{R} + \mathbf{I}$$

where $\mathbf{A}_{t+1}$ is the activation at time $t+1$ of all the neurons; $\mathbf{A}_t$ is the activation at time t of all the neurons; $\mathbf{R}$ is a vector containing each neuron's resistance, which controls the decay of its activation; and $\mathbf{I}$ is a vector of external inputs to each neuron.

3.4.3 Discussion

In many ways, Hopfield networks are very similar to the BAMs presented earlier. The BAM is an example of a matrix associative memory, and Hopfield nets are used as associative memories as well. There are, however, some significant differences between the Hopfield net and the simple matrix associative memory, particularly the continuous Hopfield net presented here.

As presented here, the Hopfield net is an analog machine. Matrix associative memories, as exemplified by BAMs, are discrete constructs. Hopfield nets have a much more sophisticated weight adjustment strategy for encoding, and they have a more sophisticated and controllable recall formula. Another minor difference is that the Hopfield net is intended as an auto-associator. Although auto-associative matrix memories could also be built, it is better to have the more sophisticated, analog associative memory be an auto-associator.

The more complicated model of the weights between neurons allows us to capture relationships beyond the purely linear ones present in simple additive matrix associative memories. With a sophisticated weight adjustment strategy, we can represent nonlinear mappings with only two layers. However, the lack of a clear-cut method for setting up the weights can be a disadvantage.

Also, capacity is an even more severe problem for the Hopfield net than for the BAM. The multimatrix BAM can overcome capacity limitations with a very clear-cut method of determining which of the recalled matrices is the correct pattern pair. There appears to be no easy way to do this with the more complicated process of Hopfield net recall (given that we are using a nontrivial recall formula, which, of course, is the reason for choosing the Hopfield model over a simple additive matrix memory).

It is doubtful that the Hopfield net should be used for any application that does not involve highly nonlinear mappings. In fact, in many of those cases, backpropagation may be a better choice. The Hopfield net's sophisticated process of weight adjustment, capabilities for encoding, and more flexible recall methods should be reserved for truly difficult problems. One example of such a problem is combinatorial optimization. This is an area where we will use Hopfield nets later on.

3.4.4 The Implementation

The implementation of the Hopfield net model follows. Very little is required beyond the generic network class. We are not about to apply this class directly anyway.

```
// HOP.HPP
// Implementation of Hopfield-Tank model

// include character vec and matrix classes
#include "net.hpp"
#include "layer.hpp"

class hop: public net {
    double initrange;
    layer *l;
public:
    hop(char *s);
    ~hop(){};
```

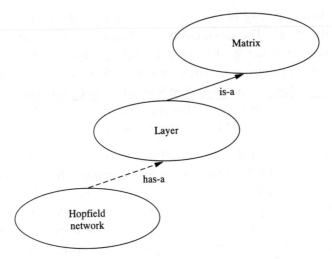

Figure 3.8 Class hierarchy for Hopfield network.

```
        void encode(const vec& A);
        vec recall(vec& A);
        int feedthru(vec& A);
};
```

Figure 3.8 presents the class hierarchy for the Hopfield net.

4

APPLICATIONS OF NEURAL NETS

■ 4.1 FORECASTING

Forecasting, at least intelligent forecasting, is predicting future events based on historical data. We choose a set of input factors that we think will be useful in predicting a set of outputs. This has typically been done with statistical methods.

We will show how they can be solved perhaps more directly, with less effort devoted to formulating the model and less time spent determining revelant input factors, with a neural network. Using a neural network, we can look at the historical data as a set of pattern associations. The input patterns are the values of all of the chosen input factors for a particular time period. The output patterns are the outputs recorded for that time period. Once the neural network is trained on the pattern associations of input and output factors for the historical data, it will "recall" output patterns when presented with input patterns. In this way, the trained neural network can predict future events based on new sets of input factors.

4.1.1 The Stock Market Predictor

The first application we present is a stock market forecaster. This is by no means an innovative use of neural nets; it is a common "example" application for neural network software packages. Applications in this and closely related fields (such as commodity market forecasting, and bond market forecasting) are common in the technical literature. Still, it is an excellent example problem that can be easily attacked with a backpropagation neural network model.

4.1.1.1 Formulating the Model

Step 1: Determine the Outputs

We will try to predict the percentage changes in price of a selection of large, prominent stocks. Notice that we are interested in price changes as opposed to predicting actual prices. This gives us a smaller range of minimum to maximum values for our neurons. Also, we look at percentage changes instead of actual dollar changes, which gives the data similar meaning for different stocks. A $1 change is significant for a $10 stock, but not for a $100 stock. A 10 percent change, on the other hand, has the same meaning regardless of the price of the stock. Using percentage changes requires a couple of extra steps in input processing, but it pays off in terms of the quality of the model.

Large, prominent stocks are likely to be more amenable to the purely technical analysis we are attempting. A good basis for picking this set of stocks is the Dow Jones 30 Industrials used to compile the Dow Jones Industrial Average. We will attempt to have the neural network predict the percentage change in the price of each of the Dow Jones 30 Industrials (Table 4.1).

Step 2:   Pick Many Input Factors

The next step is to pick as many input factors as possible that might be related to percentage changes in stock prices. Neural networks excel at sifting through a mass of data and deciding just what data is relevant and to what degree. We want to determine the many *possibly* relevant input factors and include them in the model. Those that are not relevant will simply have low connection strengths with the output neurons in the network. The drawback to using large numbers of input factors (and the reason it is generally not done in comparable statistical models) is that may inhibit performance significantly (the number of synapses will rise exponentially with the number of input neurons). There are techniques inherent in neural networks that will alleviate this problem.

We would be guilty of using smoke and mirrors if we finished the presentation of this application boasting of the effectiveness of neural networks as applied to this task but did not explain all of the components of our model. Therefore, we are about to go into a fairly long enumeration of the input factors for this neural network. Those not really concerned with the mechanics of the model should skip to step 3.

Alleviating Performance Problems

First, we can introduce parallel hardware. All the example applications in this book are implemented on a single–processor machine. However, one of the advantages of our object-oriented toolkit is ease of extensibility. All of the vector and matrix operations (which are the time-consuming portions of neural network computation) are encapsulated in the vector and matrix classes. If we move the application to a parallel machine, we need only recode the vector and matrix arithmetic operators to use the parallel instructions of the particular machine. Modern parallel processors generally provide hardware-level support (machine instructions) for most parallel arithmetic operations (for example, adding two vectors), so this recoding effort would be minimal (we would actually be reducing the amount of code). The changes would be restricted to the vector and matrix classes.

Second, we can enhance our backpropagation neural network to be a self-pruning backprop neural net. The self-pruning backprop net would remove all neurons whose synapses have very low connection strengths. An input-factor neuron that is completely irrelevant to the trained network would automatically be pruned out, reducing the number of synapses and alleviating performance problems. This approach has recently been the subject of quite a bit of research. With our object-oriented toolkit, we can simply create a new class, *prunebp*, that inherits everything from the *bp* class but changes the *train* method to include the pruning logic.

AL	Aluminum Corp. of America		MMM	Minnesota Mining and Manufacturing
ALD	Allied-Signal		MO	Philip Morris
AXP	American Express		MRK	Merck
BA	Boeing		NAV	Navistar
BS	Bethlehem Steel		PA	Primerica
CHV	Chevron		PG	Proctor & Gamble
DD	DuPont		S	Sears
EK	Eastman Kodak		T	AT&T
GE	General Electric		TX	Texaco
GM	General Motors		UK	Union Carbide
GT	Goodyear		UTX	United Technologies
IBM	International Business Machines		X	USX
IP	International Paper		XON	Exxon
KO	Coca-Cola		WX	Westinghouse
MCD	McDonald's		Z	Woolworth

Table 4.1 Dow Jones 30 industrials.

1. *Previous price fluctuations.* Some obvious input factors are the percentage changes in price for previous weeks. We have to gather the data for percentage changes anyway (since that's what we're trying to predict), and it seems reasonable that the change in a stock's price for a previous week may have some predictive power for the change in price of that stock for the upcoming week.

It is less obvious that the change in price of one stock in the previous week may affect the change in price of another stock in the upcoming week. However, since we are looking at large, prominent stocks, it may be reasonable to expect that a major fluctuation in IBM's price in a previous week, for example, may have some bearing on other Dow Jones 30 (DJ30) stocks in the upcoming week.

And it may not be only the immediately preceding week's price changes that are relevant to the upcoming week's changes. Changes in price two or three weeks earlier may also have predictive power. We already have the data, and it doesn't cost us anything to include previous weeks' changes as input factors for the coming week's prediction (except in terms of performance, and we have discussed how we will alleviate such problems). Figure 4.1 presents percent price change data by week for IBM. We will arbitrarily cut off the time window at three weeks ago (but keep this as a settable parameter in our implementation). Using three (or another preset parameter) weeks of data for each input factor will increase the number of input factors and should lead to a richer model and a more effective neural net.

2. *Volume and volatility for DJ30 stocks.* In the process of gathering the historical prices for these stocks, we automatically obtained a record of the trading volume and volatility (the high for the week minus the low for the week). The trading volume of stocks may have predictive power as well, so we will include this parameter in the model. Figures 4.2 and 4.3 present volumes and volatility data plots for IBM.

3. *Interest rates and exchange rates.* Now we need to look at macroeconomic factors that may help in predicting these stock prices. One commonly used indicator of stock price movements is interest rate. We will use changes

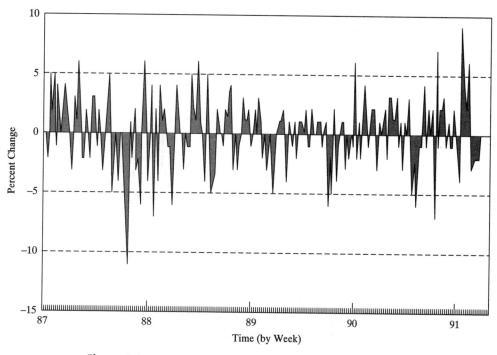

Figure 4.1 Percent price change of IBM stock (by week since 1987).

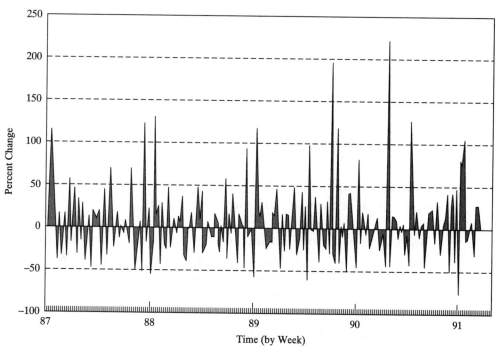

Figure 4.2 Percent change in volume of IBM stock (by week since 1987).

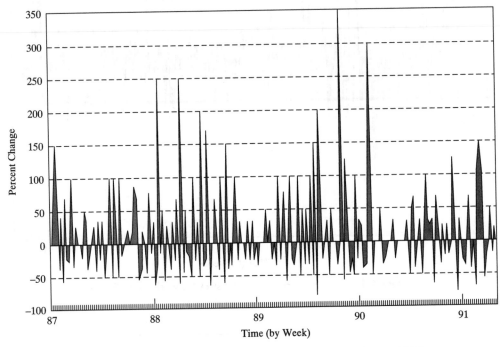

Figure 4.3 Percent change in volatility of IBM stock (by week since 1987).

(for each of the previous three weeks) in the federal funds rate, the prime rate, and the U.S. Treasury bill yields (91-day and 182-day bills) as our interest rate indicators. Another *possibly* useful class of indicators of stock price movements are currency exchange rates. Therefore, we'll incorporate the percentage changes (over the same three-week window) in the yen/dollar exchange rate and deutsche mark/dollar exchange rate into the model. Figures 4.4 and 4.5 are plots of interest rate and exchange rate changes.

4. *Stock averages.* Other macroeconomic factors are commonly used stock averages: the Dow Jones Industrial Average (DJIA), the Standard & Poor's 500 (S & P 500) stock index, and the Value Line Composite Index. Conveniently, we can compute the DJIA from information already gathered. The DJIA is simply the sum of the prices of our 30 stocks divided by 1.09. Backpropagation is supposed to be able to learn any nonlinear mapping, so theoretically, if the

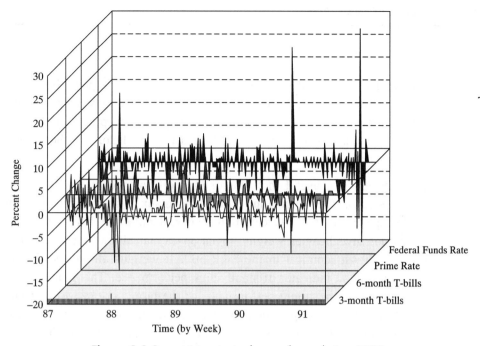

Figure 4.4 Percent interest rate changes (by week since 1987).

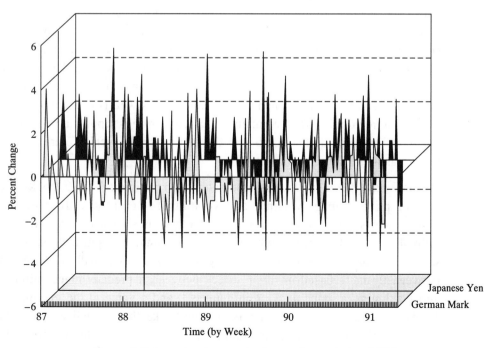

Figure 4.5 Percent exchange rate changes (by week since 1987).

average of the 30 input neurons we already have were a powerful predictor, the neural network would learn this and behave accordingly. However, it may take the network quite a while to approximate this mapping. Therefore, if it appears that changes in the Dow will be a useful predictor, we should include it explicitly as an input neuron.

The S&P 500 is a useful indicator of the performance of a wider selection of large stocks. The Value Line Composite Index is an indicator of a much broader spectrum of 1,700 common stocks. Unlike the NYSE Composite, it does not give heavier weights to larger-capitalization stocks, so it is an indicator almost identical to the S&P 500. It weights all stocks identically, making it a good indicator of small-stock performance. This index may have little bearing on the future performance of the larger stocks we are trying to predict, but it may be influential, and with a neural network model we don't worry too much about throwing in extra factors. Figure 4.6 is a plot of weekly index percent changes.

5. *Other trading-related factors.* NYSE total trading volume and overall advance and decline volumes are also input factors, as are the numbers of advances, declines, and unchanged stocks. Another factor touted as influencing stock prices is time of year. Stock prices often fall in December as people sell stock to take capital losses before the end of the tax year. The "January effect" is the phenomenon where prices rise in the month after the December fall. More subtle seasonal phenomena may exist as well (for example, prices may be more volatile when company quarterly earnings reports are issued). In our model we include the number of the month for the week we are trying to predict as a "seasonality indicator."

We now have 90 input factors associated with individual DJ30 stocks (percent of price change, volume, and volatility for each) and 16 macroeconomic factors, for a total of 106 input factors, as shown in Table 4.2. The individual stock factors overwhelm the macroeconomic input factors, and we will adjust for this during input preprocessing. All inputs will be normalized between 0 and 1 based on their values between a predetermined minimum and maximum (a value at the minimum is 0 and a value at the maximum is 1). For the macroeconomic factors, we will take the normalized value and increase it by a predetermined multiplier (we used a factor of 10 in this model).

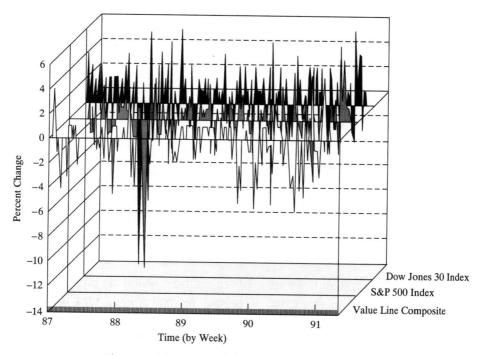

Figure 4.6 Index percent changes (by week since 1987).

We are using the data of three previous weeks as input factors for the coming week, so the number of input factors is actually three times the total of 106. For a really comprehensive model, we might want to come up with even more input factors than we have supplied here, but the model (in Table 4.2) is actually robust and effective.

The full model is included on the disk and in the listings as the DJ30 Stock Predictor. A smaller model, called IBM, is also included that attempts only to predict percent changes in the price of IBM and does not use a three-week window. This model will train in more reasonable times on machines without numeric coprocessors.

Step 3:   Choose the Neural Network Topology and Define Its Parameters

Once we know what we are trying to predict (or, in general, what outputs we're interested in) and what we base those predictions on (in general, what

Individual Stock Factors	
DJ30 percent price change	30
DJ30 volume	30
DJ30 volatility	30
Macroeconomic factors	
Interest rate measures	4
Exchange rates	2
Stock averages	3
Volume, advance, and decline measures	6
Seasonality	1
	106
	×3 weeks
	318 input factors

Table 4.2 Input factors.

our input factors are), we are ready to choose a neural net topology and define its parameters. In this case, of course, we had a good idea that we would be using backpropagation. However, in other cases it may be only after the problem is fully defined (in inputs and outputs) that we can narrow our choice of topologies to one.

For the present model backpropagation was chosen because supervised offline learning was deemed most appropriate to the application. We certainly do not want to make real-time use of the model until we are convinced completely (through offline training and testing) that it is effective. We also want the predictions to be as close as possible to the actual output, and a supervised learning algorithm should enable us to train to closer tolerances than an unsupervised one. Unsupervised learning algorithms allow us to generalize variant patterns to a set of "fuzzy" classes, which is often very useful (as we shall see), but not here. We want to narrow as much as possible the range of possible output from a widely varying input. Supervised learning allows us to ensure that we get close to the desired output and also (at least with the learning algorithms we use) that we make steady progress toward that goal. This is the property of "stability" referred to in the previous chapter.

Also, a multilayer network is crucial because any strong relationships between inputs and outputs that we discover are likely to be highly nonlinear. The stock market may not be completely efficient, but it is certainly able to defy simple linear relationships. For example, we are unlikely to find a direct, strong correlation between the percent change in the price of IBM and next week's change in the DJ30 index. Strong relationships between inputs and outputs may exist, but they are likely to be *much* more complex. Thus, we will need a multiple-layer network. As for the choice of a *three*-layer network, such a network has proven capable of capturing nonlinear relationships to an impressive level of complexity [Hecht-Nielsen 85]. More layers may prove to train faster in this case, but this application is meant to be illustrative, not optimal. Also, these applications were all developed and initially run on PCs. Even the current topology strains the limits of memory with the amount of inputs and outputs used. However, the user who wishes to experiment with these applications is encouraged to try adding another layer. An extra layer may provide additional "generalization" capability that is appropriate given the mass of input data.

Once the topology is chosen, we need to define its parameters. This is accomplished for the networks in our toolkit by editing a definition file (with a .DEF extension). This file contains the values of all the parameters, one to a line. For backpropagation, our parameters are size of the input layer of neurons, size of the hidden-layer, size of the output layer, the learn rate of the first matrix of synapses, and the learn rate of the second matrix of synapses.

The input layer consists of 318 neurons, and the output layer of 30 neurons, but the hidden-layer size is not so obvious. The hidden layer can be thought of as a sort of "feature detector," where "feature" means some type of combination of input-layer neurons. As an example, imagine a recognizer for digits hand-drawn with straight lines; the input layer might have 64 neurons representing an 8×8 array of pixels, with 1 output neuron indicating the digit recognized. There should probably be around 7 hidden-layer neurons (perhaps a couple extra) to allow detection of the seven possible straight-line "features" in these hand-drawn digits. We know this from an intuitive sense of the problem.

This decision is more difficult with our stock predictor application. Just how many "features" are there in this application? The number should lie roughly between the number of input neurons and the number of output neurons. We will initially set the number of hidden-layer neurons at 64.

The learn rate also cannot be determined optimally before we attempt to run the application, but 0.5 is a reasonable first entry (used often by McClelland in "short pattern" applications). The momentum term is 0.2 (momentum is the amount a previous weight change affects the current weight change as discussed earlier). The tolerance of our network (discussed when we introduced the backprop toolkit) is 10 percent. That is, we will accept any prediction within 10 percent of the true result as close enough. The weight range (the range within which to initialize our random weights) is between 1 and −1. Although some researchers have stated that lower initial weight values result in faster training, I have not found this to be the case.

Thus, the definition file for this application (DJ30.DEF) is as follows:

INPUTS	324
HIDDEN	64
OUTPUT	30
RATE	0.5
DECAY	0.2
TOLERANCE	0.1
EPOCH	1

Step 4:   Gather the Data

Price, volume, and volatility data for each stock is available in electronic form. So too is all the data for the indicators we have mentioned. This data will all be captured in files that have each week's input or output factor as one of the values on the line. For example, the historical data for Alcoa might appear in the file AL.DAT as follows:

870102 14508 12.778 .389 .056
870109 57845 13.667 .833 0
870116 93649 14.556 .944 .333
870123 56776 14.667 .778 .389
870130 35001 14.722 .556 .389

The date is in the first column, the volume is in the second column, the high price for the week is in the third column, the low offset from this high price is in the fourth column, and the last offset (the close at the end of the week) is in the last column. Closing price is determined by subtracting the value in the fifth column from the one in the third column. Volatility can be computed as the fourth-column (low offset) value divided by the third-column (price) value. Volume is simply the amount in the second column, with no transformations.

A utility called ADDCOL helps us take all this information and put it into the training-set fact file (DJ30.FCT). ADDCOL automatically calculates percentage differences between successive rows and puts them into the combined file if the "-%" switch is used. It has a settable "window" (with the "-Wn" switch) to allow several weeks of prior data to be used as input factors for the upcoming week. Most importantly, it performs arithmetic manipulations on combinations of columns, which is necessary for this model. The following set of commands takes the Alcoa data file and adds all of its data to the training-set fact file.

```
: adds price data by subtracting column 5 from column 3
ADDCOL DJ30.FCT AL.DAT -C3-5 -P -W3
: adds volatility data by dividing column 4 by column 3
ADDCOL DJ30.FCT AL.DAT -C4/3 -P -W3
: adds volume data as simply column 2
ADDCOL DJ30.FCT AL.DAT -C2 -P -W3
```

The training-set fact file is created by combining all the data from these files into a file with each "fact" or pattern association on a line. That is, the input pattern will be all of the input-factor numbers separated by spaces and terminated with a comma. The output factors will also appear separated by spaces and terminated with a newline character. This convention must be used by an application using our backprop toolkit. The following commands convert all of our raw data files into the training-set fact file using ADDCOL.

```
: adds price data by subtracting column 5 from column 3
FOR %%a IN (*.DAT) DO ADDCOL DJ30.FCT %a -C3-5 -P -W3
```

```
: adds volatility data by dividing column 4 by column 3
FOR %%a IN (*.DAT) DO ADDCOL DJ30.FCT %a -C4/3 -P -W3
: adds volume data as simply column 2
FOR %%a IN (*.DAT) DO ADDCOL DJ30.FCT %a -C2 -P -W3
: add index data
FOR %%a IN (*.IND) DO ADDCOL DJ30.FCT %a -C3-5 -P -W3
```

We have gone into such detail on this subject only because this type of data transformation is likely to be a large portion of the work in a neural net application of any significant size. The ADDCOL utility is included for this reason (on the accompanying disk). This task of gathering data from individual columns of many files, performing transformations on the data in these columns, and adding the results as a new column in a "master" data file to be used for training, is extremely common to neural nets using data gathered from previously existing electronic form.

Some might consider using a spreadsheet for such tasks. This will work for small applications. But for applications dealing with at least hundreds of facts (rows of data) and hundreds of input and output factors (columns of data), quick arithmetic reveals that related worksheets would be several megabytes large. Also, the data transfer effort from ASCII text to the spreadsheet and the time and effort involved in manipulating the columns in the spreadsheet make this approach impractical if we wish to be able to easily update our data or change our model. You should find ADDCOL invaluable for transforming existing data to a form usable by the neural network toolkit.

Of course, the existing data may not be in neat columnar form or may require transformations that ADDCOL does not supply. In this case, UNIX text manipulation tools such as *awk, sed,* and *lex* [Kernighan 84] should prove useful in creating files manipulable by ADDCOL or in putting columns into the training-set fact file directly. The data is gathered into a "fact file" with the application name and a .FCT extension.

However, instead of training on all of the available data, we actually want to train on only a large portion of it. We need to reserve 10 to 15 percent of the data to test our trained network. Use an editor to remove the corresponding number of rows of data from the training (.FCT) file, and make sure to copy each of these rows into the testing file (with a .TST extension).

Step 5:   Train the Network

Once we have defined our network and the data has been gathered, we are ready to train the network. The TESTBP program, built in a previous section, will take the name of our network (the base name of the definition and fact files we have built) as an argument and run the backpropagation implementation on this data. Training may take quite some time, so provision is built into the TESTBP program to save the network (to a .NET file) if we wish to suspend training and resume it later.

Step 6:   Test the Network

We then need to test the network to ensure that whatever it has learned is truly general. That is, if the weights learned from the training data will allow the network to make accurate predictions on the test data (which has not been trained on), we can be more confident that future predictions will be accurate as well. TESTBP can be invoked with the network name and the "-T" switch. In this case, it will run on the test set (the .TST file) and report on how many predictions were accurate.

Step 7:   Refine the Network

If our network turns out to be not so accurate, we may need to refine the model. This may involve coming up with new input factors, or training the network over a longer period of time (presenting it with more facts).

Of course, the behavior of some outputs may approach random noise. In this case, no amount of refining will improve the performance of the network. For example, a neural network built to predict lottery results or dice throws is unlikely to be successful no matter how many input factors we introduce or how large our training set is.

In this example the model performs well as currently defined. However, if we wanted to improve performance, we could give the network more facts, that is, train it over a longer time horizon (more rows of data). We could also add more input factors (more columns of data). We could expand the time window (to four weeks or longer). We could also add more stocks, such as those in industries related to the stocks we are trying to predict. However, we would probably not want to include these additional stocks as outputs. The more things we try to predict, the harder it is to take them all into account, so the model might actually degrade.

Step 8:   Run the Network

Once we have refined our model so that we are satisfied with our test results, we are ready to run the network to do real prediction. When TESTBP is invoked with the "-R" option, the network will run against the inputs in the .IN file and put the outputs into an .OUT file. The .OUT file will then contain the predictions based on the inputs in the .IN file.

In our stock prediction model, we might construct an input file each week with one input fact containing the data for the previous three-week window. Running TESTBP will then produce a prediction for the upcoming week's price changes.

Step 9:   Integrate the Network into a Larger System

Of course, this manual approach to running our mature network is not the ideal. One of the purposes of building this object-oriented framework is reusability and extensibility. Once we have a mature and successful neural network model for a particular application, we will probably want to incorporate it into a larger system.

Instead of manually creating input files, we can have the larger system create them. The system can then interpret the results of the output files and take appropriate actions. For example, in the stock prediction model, the large system could automate the collection of inputs from online sources. It could also make recommendations on trades by interpreting the outputs. Alternatively, it could conduct the trades itself.

The real beauty of the object-oriented approach is that we can just include a backpropagation network (or other neural network model) as an object in the larger system. All methods and data can then carry over with no extra work. However, when creating a "run-time" (as opposed to training-phase) system based on neural network objects, we may want to make a further enhancement to our neural network class.

Using the inheritance mechanism, we can create a new class, derived from any of the neural network classes presented here, that contains only the "run-time methods" (*recall* and any methods that *recall* uses). The other methods can be eliminated by redefining them as null methods. Thus, in our larger system (which is presumably created after the network has already been trained) we would include a "run-time" neural network object derived from the full neural network class.

■ 4.2 IMAGE RECOGNITION

A second major area where neural networks are often applied is image recognition. We treat each pixellated image as a pattern consisting of a sequence of either binary numbers (0 or 1 to indicate presence or absence of a pixel) or real numbers (for gray-scale or color images). We then associate each pattern with an output, which is a description of what the image represents. This might be a text description (such as "MIG-21 fighter"), or it may be simply a character, as in an optical character recognition application.

As an example of an image recognition application, we will build a handwritten-digit recognizer. We want the neural network to learn the associations between the input patterns (scanned pixellated images of handwritten digits) and output patterns (the values of the digits).

Figure 4.7 Sample handwritten digits.

One of the things demonstrated in the previous application is that backprop-agation is *slow*. To alleviate this problem, we will initially attempt to build the network with an unsupervised learning algorithm. One such network is the counterpropagation network we built in our toolkit. The LVQ layer of the CPN is particularly appropriate for its generalizing capabilities. We are likely to encounter a wide range of variation in images of handwritten digits, and it would be difficult to train on every possible variation of these images. Sam-ple handwritten digits are presented in Figure 4.7. The generalizing capability of the LVQ layer of the CPN should allow the network to make reasonable guesses at images for which it has not previously seen close matches.

4.2.1 Handwritten-Digit Recognition

Each digit image will be read in as an individual PCX file. PCX is a file format standard for graphic images introduced by Zsoft in their PC Paintbrush program. It is now supported by dozens of PC graphics packages. It is certainly the most widely used standard, despite its inelegance in comparison with formats such as TIFF. (See Craig Lindley's excellent treatment of graphic file formats in *Practical Image Processing in C,* Wiley, 1990. Also, if you are planning to do extensive work with PCX files, Genus Microprogramming's PCX Programmer's Toolkit is a useful tool, and source code is available for the routines.) Code written to train networks from PCX images should be extremely reusable. Figure 4.8 illustrates the PCX file format.

For the sake of simplicity, we assume that each digit image is in a file by itself. We scan images into paint software, cut out the digit, and save it to a PCX file. However, this is easily extensible to recognizing digit images in a larger graphic file. This could be done by having the training software look for "signposts" in the larger image indicating where the digit is located. For example, we might be processing a tax form where the numbers are placed in square boxes. If we search for the square box in the larger image, we can treat the pixels inside the square box the same as our separate PCX file images.

For digit recognition, we process the PCX file to obtain a 16×16 component image of the digit. This gives us a vector 256 neurons long. But the image in

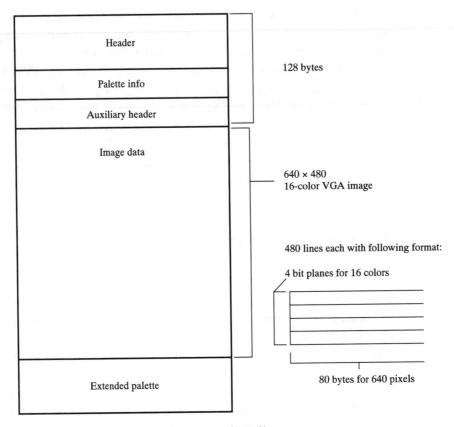

Figure 4.8 Structure of PCX files.

the PCX file is obviously greater than 16×16. In fact, it may be as large as 640×480 for VGA images, or even $1,024 \times 768$ for Super VGA or XGA images. Even for an image as small as 320×200, that's still a vector $64,000$ neurons long as our input pattern. Since we will have several hidden-layer neurons, each connected to each neuron in the input layer, we can see that we would quickly exhaust our memory for the synaptic weights ($64,000$ input neurons multiplied by 10 hidden-layer neurons is $640,000$ synaptic weights).

To get a 16×16 component image, we can simply break up the images into a 64×64 grid. A 640×480 image would result in each component being 40×30 pixels. To encode each component in our floating-point vectors, we would simply determine the number of "on" pixels in the region and divide it by the number of pixels in the region. Thus, if 400 pixels were on in the region just mentioned, the value encoded would be 0.333.

An alternative way of representing the image is to use bit vectors. C++'s operator overloading capabilities should allow us to create a bit vector class permitting access to individual bits using the array operator ("[]"). With this scheme, we could possibly handle the raw pixellated images without preprocessing them into regions. However, we are trying to reuse code as much as possible, so we would prefer to use the existing vector and matrix classes. Parameterized types could also help: we could have one generic vector and matrix class to which a parameterized type could be added. However, this is not currently in the C++ standard (as defined by the *ARM*, although there is a proposed standard, and it may reach some implementations of C++ before long). Some C++ class libraries (notably the NIH class library by Keith Gorlen) have gotten around this problem by using preprocessor macros, but this is a fairly unattractive solution (Gorlen has to resort to the macro capabilities of "m4," and the C preprocessor cannot even handle all the work involved). Also, the counterpropagation network as presented is an analog network. Perhaps it could be modified to work well as a discrete network (handling binary-valued neurons), but that is beyond the scope of this book.

The technique of handling images beyond the resolution capacity by varying the values in our pixels has precedent in the technique of "antialiasing." For some images, even VGA resolutions are insufficiently fine. For example, for a circle being drawn on a computer screen, if some pixels have their intensity reduced (turned to gray instead of black in a black-on-white-image), the circle seems smoother, as smooth as one drawn on a higher-resolution screen. We are doing a similar thing with our 16 × 16 image by using gradations across the scale of floating-point numbers.

4.2.1.1 *The Nine–Step Development Process*

Following our step-by-step process for the previous application, the outputs we are trying to predict are the values of the digits (step 1). The inputs are the vectors of 256 floating-point numbers representing the 16 × 16 component image of the digits (step 2). For the topology we have chosen the counterpropagation network, for its rapid unsupervised learning and generalization capabilities.

Choosing the size of the hidden layer is again a nontrivial problem. The hidden layer must be able to encode each possible output with one neuron. For this application, then, we would need at least 10 neurons. But we may not want to leave it at just 10, as it is possible that two (or more) dissimilar images might map to the same digit. For example, a zero drawn with a slash and one without a slash might be interpreted differently by the CPN. Using extra neurons will allow more than one neuron to encode the output zero. We will therefore create a hidden layer of 16 neurons to allow several numbers to have more than one representation. We may discover later that the CPN needs yet more hidden-layer neurons. One indicator would be images of different digits mapping to the same "winner-take-all" neuron. If this happens, we can simply change the definition and put in a larger number.

As in the previous application, we will set the parameters of learn rate, momentum, tolerance, and weight range to 0.5, 0.2, 0.1, and 1, respectively. The definition file (DIGITS.DEF) is:

```
INPUTS       256
HIDDEN       16
OUTPUTS      1
RATE         0.5
MOMENTUM     0.2
TOLERANCE    0.1
RANGE        1
```

For this application we would like to use the same standard file format for training neural networks that is used throughout our neural network toolkit. This is the file containing input-output pattern pairs. To create this file we will need to do a substantial amount of preprocessing as in the previous example (we will spare you the same level of detail, however). We need to take each PCX file, convert it to a 16×16 component image, and put this array of 256 floating-point numbers into the fact file (with a trailing comma to terminate the vector). We need to do this for each image in our training set. We can then use the ADDCOL tool to add the output part to each fact.

If we capture the images to a set of PCX files, this can be accomplished with the following steps:

```
: convert PCX files to fact file
FOR %%a IN (*.PCX) DO CVTPCX DIGITS.FCT %a
:
ADDCOL DIGITS.FCT
```

Once the data is gathered into a fact file, we will invoke TESTCPN on the DIGITS application. Once as all of our training patterns have been presented to the network, training stops. Remember, this is *unsupervised* learning. There is no need to continue to adjust the weights until our predictions are within a specified tolerance.

▪ 4.3 TEXT PROCESSING

There have been many successful applications of neural networks to text processing, including neural networks for probabilistic information retrieval [IJCNN 90]. A specific example of an information retrieval application is a simple spell checker. This is not a unique application of neural networks. Jagota and Hung of SUNY–Buffalo presented a "lexicon" (which in fact was just a spell checker) based on a Hopfield net [IJCNN 90]. Hopfield nets (as discussed earlier) are not much different from BAMs. As applied by Jagota, they are discrete additive networks with a single layer of weights (in contrast to the analog Hopfield net we use for optimization problems). They also are subject to the same capacity limitations that simple BAMs face, so it is likely that a Hopfield net approach to a spell checker would saturate almost as quickly as a BAM. The BAM System approach should overcome these limitations.

Also, many neural network-based speech recognition systems have been built. As part of these systems, a phoneme-to-spelling mapper is generally required.

A BAM System as we have described it could be used to build this, which would represent a particularly good demonstration of the BAM System's ability to overcome capacity limitations [Simpson 90].

4.3.1 BAM System Spell Checker

A "super spell checker" is a particularly good demonstration of the BAM System's strengths, since the short pattern lengths of words would quickly cause a capacity problem with a simple BAM. With a BAM System we should be able to overcome this problem and build a dictionary of realistic size.

One layer of neurons in the BAM will represent correct word spellings using sequences of letters. Each letter will be represented as a value between 1 and 26 using a five-bit code. We can then use the discrete BAM implementation with five neurons for each letter. We will allow words containing up to 10 characters, so we have a 50-neuron field for word spellings.

The other layer will represent phoneme strings. Phoneme strings are sequences of IPA (International Phonetic Alphabet) codes indicating how a word is pronounced (as you might see in a dictionary). In the files used for training, the phonemes will be represented using Standard Generalized Markup Language (SGML). SGML is the method used by the Oxford English Dictionary to store its data (which, of course, includes pronunciation strings). It will allow us to represent the many arcane symbols for phonemes in the standard ASCII character set.

For presentation to the network, each pronunciation code will be represented as a value. The range of values is sufficiently small to be represented with six bits (allowing 64 possible pronunciation codes). We will allow up to 10 pronunciation codes per word, so that we will have 60 neurons in this layer.

Notice that we have not explicitly specified any inputs or outputs. A BAM, of course, is bidirectional, so we have no strict inputs or outputs. We can give this BAM application a word, and it will return a pronunciation as well as a (possibly corrected) word. If we give it a pronunciation, it will return a word and a (possibly corrected) pronunciation. The *recall* operation returns a pattern pair instead of just one pattern, and we can present it with either type of pattern that the BAM handles.

Of course, if the system is embedded in a larger application, there may very well be one end that is considered an input. In the spell checker, we will generally supply the word spelling as an input. The output will be both the word spelling (possibly corrected) and its pronunciation (which may be ignored by the spell checker application). That is, the word spelling is both the input and the output, as used in the BAM implementation of the spell checker.

Of course, the same BAM (the same information stored in the BAM System weights) could also be used by a speech recognition system. The acoustic patterns could be parsed into phonemes and presented to the BAM System. The correct word would then be recalled (and typed into a word processor, for example). In this case, the phonemes would be considered inputs, and spellings would be considered outputs.

There are no other parameters that must be decided upon for the BAM. The learn rate is by definition 1, and momentum is not relevant (it is 0). We are not performing supervised learning, so there is no tolerance factor. Our definition file (SPELL.DEF) is therefore just:

> INPUTS 40 (size of word layer)
> OUTPUTS 30 (size of phoneme string layer)

The data will be in a fact file (SPELL.FCT), with each word and its phoneme on a separate line. But the BAM System class we have built cannot work directly from words and phonemes. A new class, *spellbam*, is derived from the BAM System class. The *spellbam* class has everything that *bam_system* had (all of its data and methods); it simply overrides the *encode* and *recall* methods to allow encoding and recall of words. The *encode* method invokes conversion methods to form a binary vector pair from a word (consisting of spelling and pronunciation strings) and calls the BAM System *encode* method to encode the binary vector pair into the BAM. *Recall* converts a word to a binary vector pair and invokes the BAM System *recall* method.

The returned vector pair is then converted to a word (spelling-pronunciation pair). Following is the definition for the *spellbam* class.

```
class spellbam: public bam_system {
        public:

                spellbam(){}
                ~spellbam(){}
                void encode(word& w);
                word& recall(word& w);

        }
```

The *word* class is used to store both a word's spelling and its pronunciation. The *makevec* method will convert these to a vector pair. The word constructor will build a word from a vector pair. The class definition is:

```
class word {
        friend operator>>(istream& s,word& w);
                unsigned char *spell;
                unsigned char *pronounce;
        public:
                word();
                word(vecpair& v);
                ~word(){};
                vecpair& makevec();

        }
```

Using C++'s inheritance mechanism, we have extended our abstract BAM System into a working spell checker with very little modification. In the two previous applications, we did not even create a new class; we just ran each neural net's test program with data files constructed for the application. The work of making the application "talk to the real world" was done by processing data files into the format expected by the neural net toolkit. For the spell checker, this would involve a quite complicated file conversion process to convert files of words and phonemes to files of 0s and 1s. The appropriate file representation is the actual words and phonemes. The conversion to binary strings should be done on the fly. This also provides an example of how C++

and inheritance allow us to extend our toolkit into a working application with very little programming.

■ 4.4 OPTIMIZATION

Neural networks have often been formulated to solve difficult (for the most part, NP-complete) optimization problems. When we refer to optimization here, we refer to the process of finding the "best" (optimal) solution among many possible alternatives. Generally, a problem not an optimization problem if we can practically enumerate all the alternatives and apply an evaluation formula to each one. Optimization problems typically require some form of algorithm to arrive at the best alternative.

The branch of mathematics and science most concerned with optimization problems is operations research (OR). OR problems are typically formulated as minimizing or maximizing a formula subject to a set of constraints. If we are minimizing something, the problem is often referred to as "cost minimization," although the entity we are minimizing may not be measured in money. The constraints are represented as a set of inequalities establishing bounds on the variables (or a subset of the variables) in the cost formula. If these bounds were not there, it would be a very simple matter to minimize the cost function.

Problems with a limited number of constraints and variables can be solved using a mathematical algorithm. A popular example of such an algorithm is the simplex method, which defines the bounds as a set of vectors in n-space (where n is the number of variables). These vectors define a surface in n-space containing the solution set. If the value of each variable in the proposed solution is within the bounds, then it is a feasible solution. If any dimension or variable is outside the bounds, then it is an infeasible solution.

If the set of vectors implied by the constraints suggests an unclosed region in n-space, then the problem probably is "unbounded." For example, if there were no minimum for a particular variable in any of the constraints, and that variable is used in the cost function, then we could simply reduce the amount of that variable infinitely to minimize the cost. If we have a bounded problem, our optimal solution must lie on the surface of the solution set. In fact, it must lie at one of the vertices where two or more bounds meet.

To use the simplex method, we start with a point where one dimension is zero on the surface of the solution set, and we move from one vertex to another until there is no further improvement in the cost function value. The simplex method works admirably for many problems, but for very large problems it can be very slow. One speedup proposed for such problems is to start with an interior point close to the optimal vertex and move outward. However, this is difficult, and it will still be time-consuming for extremely large problems.

Harking back to our earlier discussion about the limits of single-processor machines, the straight-line algorithms such as simplex inevitably reach the point where the solution time is no longer reasonable. Attempts have been made to code implementations of the simplex algorithm for vector processors (SIMD machines). However, speedups greater than 25 percent on a cross section of large benchmarks have not been realized. There are just too many places in the simplex algorithm that require sequential examination of data values. To be fair, there are also many places in the algorithm that should be able to use vector instructions because the data values could all be operated on at the same time. Better (larger-capacity) SIMD processors may increase speed somewhat more, possibly up to 100% faster (a reasonable goal). However, the machines are quite expensive, and we will certainly see no jump in the class of problems that can be solved with such an increase.

Prospects for exploitation of MIMD using simplex or its variants are even bleaker. These algorithms simply are not parallel algorithms. They cannot address the problem in a parallel way. However, neural nets can. Neural networks have often been applied to optimization problems with a good deal of success. One of the first applications of neural networks to optimization was Hopfield and Tank's solution of the traveling salesman problem.

4.4.1 Traveling Salesman Problem

One of the first applications that Hopfield and Tank envisioned for their model (the Hopfield net described in the previous chapter) was the solution,

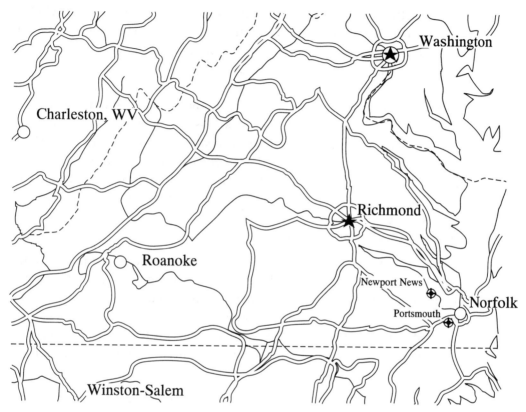

Figure 4.9 Map of cities for traveling salesman problem.

	Charleston	Norfolk	Richmond	Roanoke	Washington
Charleston	X	405	309	180	342
Norfolk	405	X	92	250	189
Richmond	309	92	X	185	105
Roanoke	180	250	185	X	233
Washington	342	189	105	233	X

Figure 4.10 Distances for traveling salesman problem.

or attempted solution, of NP-complete optimization problems [Hopfield 85]. One such problem is the traveling salesman problem, or TSP, which attempts to find the shortest path through n cities, where each city is visited exactly once (see Figure 4.9). This is a classic OR problem that has often been solved with the simplex method. The problem is quite common in practical situations and has been researched quite thoroughly, but it remains challenging. The solution becomes intractable very quickly as the number of cities (or nodes to visit) increases, since the number of possible paths is $n!/2n$. Generally, a branch-and-bound method is used with some sort of heuristic to prune the prohibitively large search tree. Even with these techniques, however, large-scale applications of this type are extremely compute-intensive. If there were any way to formulate a PDP approach to solving this problem, we could probably benefit from the inherent parallelism.

One way in which a tour of all cities can be represented is as a matrix, where a 1 appears at the intersection of the row representing the city and the column representing the order visited. A complete tour should have a 1 in each row and a 1 in each column, but no more than one in each row or column. The optimal tour is indicated by the minimum total distance traveled, which is computed by adding the distances between cities. Such a matrix might take the form shown in Figure 4.10.

Hopfield proposes an energy function that will be minimized on an optimal solution of the problem:

$$
\begin{aligned}
E = {}& A/2 \sum_X \sum_i \sum_{j \neq i} OUT_{Xi} OUT_{Xj} \\
& + B/2 \sum_X \sum_i \sum_{j \neq i} OUT_{Xi} OUT_{Yi} \\
& + C/2 [(\sum_X \sum_i OUT_{Xi}) - n]^2 \\
& + D/2 \sum_X \sum_i \sum_{j \neq i} d_{XY} OUT_{Xi}(OUT_{Y,i+1} OUT_{Y,i-1})
\end{aligned}
$$

where A, B, C, and D are constants and where d represents distances between cities. The first and second terms prevent visiting a city twice, and the third ensures that we visit each city. The fourth term penalizes long tours to create an incentive for shorter tours.

The Hopfield net that solves this problem has a neuron for each element of the matrix, and the neurons are fully interconnected. Thus, the synapses will be essentially a matrix of matrices (a four-dimensional matrix). To get the Hopfield net to minimize this energy function, we create a set of weights in this four-dimensional matrix as follows:

$$\mathbf{w}_{xi,yj} = -A\delta_{xy}(1 - \delta_{ij}) - B\delta_{ij}(1 - \delta_{xy}) - C - Dd_{xy}(\delta_{j,i+1} + \delta_{j,i-1})$$

where $\delta_{ij} = 1$ if $i = j$ and is 0 otherwise.

4.4.1.1 The Implementation

In our application we put these weight formulas into the network manually by reading the distances from a matrix. Then simply running the network will result in the optimal route. Thus, our TSP class only has two major methods: *setweights* and *run*; there is no *train* method *per se*. We have simply taken the Hopfield net approach of handcrafted weight adjustment formula for training to the extreme, by simply setting the weights to appropriate values. However, we do not try to pretend that this is a true training phase, so the method is called *setweights*. Still, it presents a good example of how the Hopfield net can capture relationships that are much too complicated and nonlinear for a two-layer network to absorb.

Following is the definition for the TSP class that solves the traveling salesman problem.

```
// TSP.HPP
// Implementation of the traveling salesman problem
// Using Hopfield net
#include "vecmat.hpp"
#include "math.h"
#define MAXVEC 8
#define delt(x,y) (((x)==(y))?1:0)
class tsp: public hop {
        char name[9];
        int n;
```

```
            float W[MAXVEC][MAXVEC][MAXVEC][MAXVEC];
            matrix *d;
            double A,B,C,D;
            void setweights();
    public:
            tsp(char *s);
            ~tsp(){};
            void run();
            matrix feed(matrix& M);
            double excitation(double net);
    };
```

APPENDIX I LISTINGS FOR NEURAL NET CLASS LIBRARY

■ I.1 THE MAKEFILE (BUILDING THE TOOLKIT)

Before presenting any of the individual listings, we present a makefile that will be used to construct all of the different neural net models in the library. The makefile is coded for PolyMake but should work with any true Unix-style make (Microsoft Make does not fit into that category). Several C++ compilers had to be supported; no one particular compiler's make could be assumed to be a standard. As noted in the comments, the makefile can be invoked with the COMP macro set to a different compiler. PolyMake allows us to do this easily.

However, the top of the makefile must be fairly complex to be able to handle this array of compilers. To quickly see the dependencies involved in building any of the applications, skip to the end of the NETS.MAK file.

```
#
#                    NETS.MAK
#
#           Make file for NET class library
#
# For Borland C++ 2.0, Turbo C++, and Zortech C++ 2.0 and greater
# Invoke with "make COMP=ztc nets.mak" for Zortech compile
# Invoke with "make COMP=tcc nets.mak" for Turbo C++ compile
#
# PolyMake 3.0 make file
# or other Unix-compatible make (not Microsoft make)
# Copyright (c) 1991, Adam Blum

# default to Borland C++
COMP=bcc
MODEL=l
OPT=t

%if $(COMP)=="bcc"
# change this to identify your own directory
ROOTDIR=c:\bc
LIBDIR=$(ROOTDIR)\lib
CC=$(COMP) -c -m$(MODEL) -I$(ROOTDIR)\include -L$(LIBDIR) -G -v
```

```
LINK=tlink -v
OBJ=$(LIBDIR)\c0$(MODEL)
LIBS=$(LIBDIR)\c$(MODEL)+$(LIBDIR)\math$(MODEL)+$(LIBDIR)\emu

%else
%if $(COMP)=="tcc"
# change this to identify your own directory
ROOTDIR=c:\tc
LIBDIR=$(ROOTDIR)\lib
CC=tcc -v -c -m$(MODEL) -I$(INCDIR) -O$(OPT)
LINK=tlink -v
OBJ=$(LIBDIR)\c0$(MODEL)
LIBS=$(LIBDIR)\c$(MODEL)+$(LIBDIR)\math$(MODEL)+$(LIBDIR)\emu

%else
%if $(COMP)=="ztc"
# change this to identify your own directory
ROOTDIR=c:\zc
LIBDIR=$(ROOTDIR)\lib
INCDIR=$(ROOTDIR)\include
CC=ztc -c -m$(MODEL) -I$(INCDIR) -g
LINK=blink /CO
OBJ=
LIBS=$(LIBDIR)\pl$(MODEL)+$(LIBDIR)\zl$(MODEL)+$(LIBDIR)\iostr_l.lib
%endif
%endif
%endif

.cpp.obj:
        :$(CC) $< > $*.err

.obj.exe:
        :$(LINK) $**$(OBJ),,,$(LIBS); >link.err

testbp.exe: testbp.obj bp.obj vecmat.obj

testcpn.exe: testcpn.obj cpn.obj vecmat.obj

testhop.exe: testhop.obj hop.obj cvecmat.obj

tsp.exe: tsp.obj vecmat.obj
```

■ 1.2 VECTOR AND MATRIX CLASSES

1.2.1 VECMAT.HPP

```cpp
/////////////////////////////////////////////////////
// VECMAT.HPP
// Vector and matrix classes
// Copyright (c) 1990, Adam S. Blum


#include<stdlib.h>
#include<io.h>
#include<conio.h>
#include<fcntl.h>
#include<stdio.h>
#include<string.h>
#include<limits.h>
#include<ctype.h>
#include<math.h>
#include<time.h>
#include<float.h>
#include<sys\stat.h>

#ifdef _TURBOC_
#include<alloc.h>
#elif defined(_ZTC_)
#include<dos.h>
#endif

#include<iostream.h>
#include<fstream.h>
#include<iomanip.h>

// C++ doesnt have min/max
#define max(a,b)        (((a) > (b)) ? (a) : (b))
#define min(a,b)        (((a) < (b)) ? (a) : (b))
```

```cpp
#include"debug.h"
double logistic(double activation);
// will be changed to values much higher than these
const ROWS=64;   // number of rows (length of first pattern)
const COLS=64;   // number of columns (length of second pattern)
const MAXVEC=64; // default size of vectors

class matrix;
class vec {
        friend ostream& operator<<(ostream& s,vec& v1);
        #ifdef _TURBOC_
        friend ostream far& operator<<(ostream far& s,vec far& v1);
        #endif
        friend class matrix;
        friend istream& operator>>(istream& s,vec& v1);
                int n;
                float *v;
        public:
                vec(int size=MAXVEC,int val=0); // constructor
                ~vec(); // destructor
                vec(vec &v1); // copy-initializer
                int length();
                float distance(vec& A);
                vec& normalize();
                vec& normalizeon();
                vec& scale(vec& minvec,vec& maxvec);
                // dot product of vector and complement
                float d_logistic();
                float maxval();
                vec& garble(float noise);
                vec& operator=(const vec& v1); // vector assignment
                vec operator+(const vec& v1);   // vector addition
                vec operator+(const float d);
                // vector additive-assignment
                vec& operator+=(const vec& v1);
                // supplied for completeness,
                // but we don't use this now
                // vector multiply by constant
                vec& operator*=(float c);
                // vector transpose multiply needs access to v array
                int operator==(const vec& v1);
```

```
        float operator[](int x);
        int vec::maxindex();
        vec& getstr(char *s);
        void putstr(char *s);

        vec operator-(const vec& v1);     // subtraction
        vec operator-(const float d);     // subtraction
        float operator*(const vec& v1);   // dot-product
        vec operator*(float c);  // multiply by constant
        vec& sigmoid();
        vec& set(int i, float f=0);
                int load (FILE *f);
                int save (FILE *f);
}; //vector class

class vecpair;

class matrix {
        friend class hop;
        friend class tsp;
        friend ostream& operator<<(ostream& s,matrix& m1);
        friend istream& operator>>(istream& s,matrix& m1);
        protected:
                float **m; // the matrix representation
                int r,c; // number of rows and columns
        public:
                // constructors
                matrix(int n=ROWS,int p=COLS,float range=0);
                matrix(int n,int p,float value,float range);
                matrix(int n,int p,char *fn);
                matrix(const vecpair& vp);
                matrix(matrix& m1); // copy-initializer
                ~matrix();
                int depth();
                int width();
                matrix& operator=(const matrix& m1);
                matrix& operator+(const matrix& m1);
```

```
                vec operator*(vec& v1);
                vec colslice(int col);
                vec rowslice(int row);
                void insertcol(vec& v,int col);
                void insertrow(vec& v,int row);
                int closestcol(vec& v);
                int closestcol(vec& v,int *wins,float scaling);
                int closestrow(vec& v);
                int closestrow(vec& v,int *wins,float scaling);
                int load(FILE *f);
                int save(FILE *f);

                matrix& operator+=(const matrix& m1);
                matrix& operator*(const float d);
                matrix& operator*=(const float d);
                void initvals(const vec& v1,const vec& v2,
                      const float rate=1.0,const float momentum=0.0);
                float getval (int row, int col);
                void setval (int row, int col, float val);

}; // matrix class

class vecpair {
        friend class matrix;
        friend ifstream& operator>>(ifstream& s,vecpair& v1);
        friend ostream& operator<<(ostream& s,vecpair& v1);
        friend matrix::matrix(const vecpair& vp);
                // flag signalling whether encoding succeeded
                int flag;
        public:
                vec *a;
                vec *b;
                vecpair(int n=ROWS,int p=COLS); // constructor
                vecpair(vec& A,vec& B);
                vecpair(const vecpair& AB); // copy initializer
                ~vecpair();
                vecpair& operator=(const vecpair& v1);
                int operator==(const vecpair& v1);
                vecpair& scale(vecpair& minvecs,vecpair& maxvecs);
};
```

1.2.2 VECMAT.CPP

```cpp
/////////////////////////////////////////////////////////////
// VECMAT.CPP
// vector and matrix class methods
// Copyright (c) 1990, Adam Blum

#include"vecmat.hpp"

/////////////////////////////////////
// vector class member functions

vec::vec(int size,int val)
{
        v = new float[n=size];
        for(int i=0;i<n;i++)
                v[i]=val;
} // constructor

vec::~vec() { delete v;} // destructor
vec::vec(vec& v1) // copy-initializer
{
        v=new float[n=v1.n];
        for(int i=0;i<n;i++)
                v[i]=v1.v[i];
}

vec& vec::operator=(const vec& v1)
{
        delete v;
        v=new float[n=v1.n];
        for(int i=0;i<n;i++)
                v[i]=v1.v[i];
        return *this;
}

vec vec::operator+(const vec& v1)
{
        vec sum(v1.n);
```

```
        for(int i=0;i<v1.n;i++)
                  sum.v[i]=v1.v[i]+v[i];
        return sum;
}
vec vec::operator+(const float d)
{
        vec sum(n);
        for(int i=0;i<n;i++)

                   sum.v[i]=v[i]+d;
        return sum;

}



vec& vec::operator+=(const vec& v1)
{
        for(int i=0;i<v1.n;i++)
                v[i]+=v1.v[i];
        return *this;

}

float vec::operator*(const vec& v1) // dot-product
{
        float sum=0;
        for(int i=0;i<min(n,v1.n);i++)
                sum+=(v1.v[i]*v[i]);
        //D(cout << "dot product " << *this << v1 << sum << "\n"; )
        return sum;

}

int vec::operator==(const vec& v1)
{
        if(v1.n!=n)return 0;
        for(int i=0;i<min(n,v1.n);i++){
                if(v1.v[i]!=v[i]){
                        return 0;
                }
        }
        return 1;

}
```

```
float vec::operator[](int x)
{
        if(x<length() && x>=0)
                return v[x];
        else
                cerr << "vec index out of range";
        return 0;
}

int vec::length(){return n;} // length method

vec& vec::garble(float noise) // corrupt vector w/random noise
{
        time_t t;
        time(&t);
        srand((unsigned)t);
        for(int i=0;i<n;i++){
                if((rand()%10)/10<noise)
                        v[i]=1-v[i];
        }
        return *this;
}



vec& vec::normalize() // normalize by length
{
        for(int i=0;i<n;i++)
                v[i]/=n;
        return *this;
}
vec& vec::normalizeon() //normalize by nonzero elements
{
        int on=0;
        for(int i=0;i<n;i++)
                if(v[i])
                        on++;
        for(i=0;i<n;i++)
                v[i]/=on;
        return *this;
}
```

```
float vec::maxval() // returns maximum ABSOLUTE value

        float mx=0;
        for(int i=0;i<n;i++)
                if(fabs(v[i])>mx){
                        mx=fabs(v[i]);

                }
        return mx;
vec& vec::scale(vec& minvec,vec& maxvec)
{
        for(int i=0;i<n;i++){
                if(v[i]<minvec.v[i])
                        v[i]=0;
                else if(v[i]>maxvec.v[i])
                        v[i]=1;
                else if((maxvec.v[i]-minvec.v[i])==0)
                        v[i]=1;
                else
                        v[i]=(v[i]-minvec.v[i])
                                /(maxvec.v[i]-minvec.v[i]);

        }
        return *this;

}
float vec::d_logistic() // returns vec * (1-vec)
{
        float sum=0.0;
        for(int i=0;i<n;i++)
                sum+=(v[i]*(1-v[i]));
        return sum;

}


// Euclidean distance function ||A-B||
float vec::distance(vec& A)
{
        float sum=0,d;
        for(int i=0;i<n;i++){
                d=v[i]-A.v[i];
                if(d)sum+=pow(d,2);

        }
        return sum?pow(sum,0.5):0;

}
```

```
// index of the highest item in vector
int vec::maxindex()
{
        int idx,i;
        float mx=
        for(i=0,mx=-FLT_MAX;i<n;i++)

                if(v[i]>mx){
                        mx=v[i];
                        idx=i;
                    }
        return idx;
}


double logistic(double activation)
{

//* These underflow limits were copied from McClelland's bp
//implementation. We had problems with underflow with numbers that
//should have been small enough in magnitude. McClelland seems to have
//encountered this and established the numbers below as reasonable
//limits. - AB */

        if(activation>11.5129)
                return 0.99999;
        if(activation<-11.5129)
                return 0.00001;
        return 1.0/(1.0+exp(-activation));
}

vec& vec::getstr(char *s)
{
        for(int i=0;i<MAXVEC&&s[i];i++){
                if(isalpha(s[i]))
                        v[toupper(s[i])-'A']=1;
        }
        return *this;
}
```

```
void vec::putstr(char *s)
{
        int ct=0;
        for(int i=0;i<26;i++)
                if(v[i]>0.9)
                        s[ct++]='A'+i;
}

vec vec::operator-(const vec& v1)
{
        vec diff(n);
        for(int i=0;i<n;i++)
                diff.v[i]=v[i]-v1.v[i];
        return diff;
}

vec vec::operator-(const float d)// subtraction of constant
{
        vec diff(n);
        for(int i=0;i<n;i++)
                diff.v[i]=v[i]-d;
        return diff;
}

vec vec::operator*(float c)
{
        vec prod(length());
        for(int i=0;i<prod.n;i++)
                prod.v[i]=v[i]*c;
        return prod;
}

vec& vec::operator*=(float c)
{
        for(int i=0;i<n;i++)
                v[i]*=c;
        return *this;
} // vector multiply by constant

vec& vec::sigmoid()
{
        for(int i=0;i<n;i++)
```

```
                    v[i]=(float)logistic((double)v[i]);
            return *this;
}
vec& vec::set(int i, float f)
{
            v[i]=f;
            return *this;
}
istream& operator>>(istream& s,vec& v1)
// format: list of floating point numbers followed by ','
{
        float d;int i=0,c;
        for(;;){
                    s>>d;
                    if(s.eof())
                            return s;
                    if(s.fail()){
                            s.clear();
                            do
                                    c=s.get();
                    while(c!=',');
                    return s;
            }
            v1.v[i++]=d;
            if(i==v1.n){
                do
                                    c=s.get();
                    while(c!=',');
                    return s;
            }
        }
}
ostream& operator<<(ostream& s,vec& v1)
// format: list of floating-point numbers followed by ','
{
        s.precision(2);
        for(int i=0;i<v1.n;i++)
                s << v1[i] <<" ";
        s << ",";
        return s;
}
```

```
int vec::save(FILE *f) // save binary values of matrix from specified file
{
    int success=1;
    for(int i=0;i<n;i++)
        if(fwrite(&(v[i]),sizeof(v[i]),1,f) < 1)
            success=0;
    return success;
}

int vec::load(FILE *f) // load binary values of vector from specified file
{
    int success=1;
    for(int i=0;i<n;i++)
        if(fread(&(v[i]),sizeof(v[0]),1,f) < 1)
            success=0;
    return success;
}

//////////////////////////////////
// matrix   member functions
matrix::matrix(int n,int p,float range)
{
        int i,j,rnd;time_t t;
        int pct,val;

        m=new float *[n];
        if(range){
                time(&t);
                srand((unsigned)t);
        }
        for(i=0;i<n;i++){
                m[i]=new float[p];
                for(j=0;j<p;j++){
                        if(range){
                                rnd=rand();
                                pct=(int)(range * 100.0);
                                val= rnd % pct;
                                m[i][j]= (float) val / 100.0 ;
                                if(range<0)
                                        m[i][j] = fabs(range)
                                                - (m[i][j] * 2.0);
                }
```

```
                       else
                                  m[i][j]=0;
                  }
           }
        r=n;
        c=p;
}
matrix::matrix(int n,int p,float value,float range)
{
        int i,j;
        m=new float *[n];
        for(i=0;i<n;i++){
                m[i]=new float[p];
                for(j=0;j<p;j++)
                        m[i][j]=value;
        }
        r=n;
        c=p;
}
matrix::matrix(int n,int p,char *fn)
{
        int i,j,rnd;time_t t;
        m=new float *[n];
        for(i=0;i<n;i++){
                m[i]=new float[p];
        }
        r=n;
        c=p;
        ifstream in(fn,ios::in);
        in >> *this;
}

matrix::matrix(const vecpair& vp)
{
        r=vp.a->length();
        c=vp.b->length();
        m=new float *[r];
        for(int i=0;i<r;i++){
                m[i]=new float[c];
                for(int j=0;j<c;j++)
                        m[i][j]=vp.a->v[i]*vp.b->v[j];
        }
}// constructor
```

```
matrix::matrix(matrix& m1) // copy-initializer
{
        //D(cout << "matrix copy-initializer\n";)
        r=m1.r;
        c=m1.c;
        m=new float *[r];
        for(int i=0;i<r;i++){
                m[i]=new float[c];
                for(int j=0;j<c;j++)
                        m[i][j]=m1.m[i][j];
        }
}


matrix::~matrix()

{
        for(int i=0;i<r;i++)
                delete m[i];
        delete m;
} // destructor

matrix& matrix::operator=(const matrix& m1)
{
        for(int i=0;i<r;i++)
                delete m[i];
        r=m1.r;
        c=m1.c;
        m=new float*[r];
        for(i=0;i<r;i++){
                m[i]=new float[c];
                for(int j=0;j<r;j++)
                        m[i][j]=m1.m[i][j];
        }
        return *this;
}


matrix& matrix::operator+(const matrix& m1)
{
        int i,j;
        matrix sum(r,c);
        for(i=0;i<r;i++)
                for(j=0;j<r;j++)
```

```
                                    sum.m[i][j]=m1.m[i][j]+m[i][j];
            return sum;
}
matrix& matrix::operator*(const float d)
{
        int i,j;
        for(i=0;i<r;i++)
                for(j=0;j<c;j++)
                        m[i][j]*=d;
        return *this;
}


vec matrix::colslice(int col)
{
        vec temp(r);

        for(int i=0;i<r;i++)
                temp.v[i]=m[i][col];
        return temp;
}
vec matrix::rowslice(int row)
{
        vec temp(c);
        for(int i=0;i<c;i++)
                temp.v[i]=m[row][i];
        return temp;
}


void matrix::insertcol(vec& v,int col)
{
        for(int i=0;i<v.n;i++)
                m[i][col]=v.v[i];
}


void matrix::insertrow(vec& v,int row)
{
        for(int i=0;i<v.n;i++)
                m[row][i]=v.v[i];
}


int matrix::depth(){return r;}
int matrix::width(){return c;}
```

```
float matrix::getval(int row,mt col)
{
        return m[row][col];
}
void matrix::setval(int row,int col, float val)
{
        m[row][col]=val;
}


int matrix::closestcol(vec& v)
{
        int mincol;
        float d;
        float mindist=INT_MAX;
        vec w(r);
        for(int i=0;i<c;i++){
                w=colslice(i);
                if( (d=v.distance(w)) < mindist){
                        mindist=d;
                        mincol=i;
                    }
            }

        return mincol;
}
int matrix::closestrow(vec& v)
{
        int minrow;
        float d;
        float mindist=INT_MAX;
        vec w(c);
        for(int i=0;i<r;i++){
                w=rowslice(i);
                if( (d=v.distance(w)) < mindist){
                        mindist=d;
                        minrow=i;
                    }
            }
        return minrow;
}
```

```
int matrix::closestrow(vec& v,int *wins,float scaling)
{
        int minrow;
        float d;
        float mindist=INT_MAX;
        vec w(c);
        for(int i=0;i<r;i++){
                w=rowslice(i);
                d=v.distance(w);
                d*=(1+((float)wins[i]*scaling));
                if( d < mindist){
                        mindist=d;
                        minrow=i;
                }
        }
        return minrow;
}
// save binary values of matrix to specified raw file
int matrix::save(FILE *f)
{
        int success=1;
        for(int i=0;i<r;i++)
                for(int j=0;j<c;j++)
                        if(f write(success=0;&(m[i][j]),sizeof(m[0][0],1,f)<1))

        return success;
}


// load binary values of matrix from specified raw file
int matrix::load(FILE *f)
{
        int success=1;
        for(int i=0;i<r;i++)
                for(int j=0;j<c;j++)
                        if(f read(&(m[i][j]),sizeof(m[0][0]),1,f) <0)
                                success=0;
        return success;
}
```

```
matrix& matrix::operator+=(const matrix& m1)
{
        int i,j;
        for(i=0;i<r&&i<m1.r;i++)
                for(j=0;j<c&&j<m1.c;j++)
                        m[i][j]+=(m1.m[i][j]);
        return *this;
}

matrix& matrix::operator*=(const float d)
{
        int i,j;
        for(i=0;i<r;i++)
                for(j=0;j<c;j++)
                        m[i][j]*=d;
        return *this;
}

vec matrix::operator*(vec& v1)
{
        vec temp(v1.n==r?c:r),temp2(v1.n==r?r:c);
        for(int i=0;i<((v1.n==r)?c:r);i++){
                if(v1.n==r)
                        temp2=colslice(i);
                else
                        temp2=rowslice(i);
                temp.v[i]=v1*temp2;
        }
        return temp;
}

void matrix::initvals(const vec& v1,const vec& v2,
                        const float rate,const float momentum)
{
        for(int i=0;i<r;i++)
                for(int j=0;j<c;j++)
                        m[i][j]=(m[i][j]*momentum)+((v1.v[i]*v2.v[j])*rate);
}
```

```
ostream& operator<<(ostream& s,matrix& m1)
// print a matrix
{
        for(int i=0;i<m1.r;i++){
                for(int j=0;j<m1.c;j++){
                        s << m1.m[i][j] << " ";
                }
                s << "\n";
        }
        return s;
}

istream& operator>>(istream& s,matrix& m1)
{
        for(int i=0;i<m1.r;i++){
                for(int j=0;j<m1.c;j++){
                        s >> m1.m[i][j];
                }
        }
        return s;

}

///////////////////////////////////////////
// vecpair   member functions
// constructor
vecpair::vecpair(int n,int p)
{
        a=new vec(n);b=new vec(p);
}

vecpair::vecpair(vec& A,vec& B)
{
        a=new vec(A.length());
        *a=A;
        b=new vec(B.length());
        *b=B;
}

vecpair::vecpair(const vecpair& AB)
{
        *this=vecpair(*(AB.a),*(AB.b));
}
```

```
vecpair::~vecpair() {
        delete a; delete b;
} // destructor

vecpair& vecpair::operator=(const vecpair& v1)
{
        *a=*(v1.a);

        *b=*(v1.b);
        return *this;
}

vecpair& vecpair::scale(vecpair& minvecs,vecpair& maxvecs)
{
        a->scale(*(minvecs.a),*(maxvecs.a));
        b->scale(*(minvecs.b),*(maxvecs.b));
        return *this;
}

int vecpair::operator==(const vecpair& v1)
{
        return  (*a == *(v1.a)) && (*b == *(v1.b));
}

ifstream& operator>>(ifstream& s,vecpair &v1)
// input a vector pair
{
        s>>*(v1.a)>>*(v1.b);
        return s;
}

ostream& operator<<(ostream& s,vecpair &v1)
// print a vector pair
{
        return s<<*(v1.a)<<*(v1.b)<<"\n";
}
```

■ 1.3 NEURAL NETWORK CLASS

1.3.1 NET.HPP

```
// NET.HPP
// Header file for abstract neural network base class
// To be used as parent to specific neural network implementations.
// The encode and recall methods are defined as pure virtual functions,
// making this an abstract class that can never be instantiated.
// Details of encode and recall must depend on the topology
// itself.  However, the methods ''train,'' ''test,'' and ''run''
// can be defined since they are substantively the same for each
// of the classes. The constructor can be defined and will be used
// by child classes in their own constructors to instantiate
// common elements of derived classes.

#include "vecmat.hpp"

// parameter class used to point to variable to be initialized
// and specify string to be used in definition file to initialize it

enum vartype {real,integer,string};
const NAMELEN=16;

/////////////////////////////////
// Parameter table functions

int readparms(int n,PARM *p,char *name)
{
   char fn[16];
   sprintf(fn,"%s.DEF",name);
   ifstream def(fn,ios::in);
   if(!def){
      cerr << "Failed to find definition file.\n";
      return 0;
   }
   while   (readparm(def,n,p) && !def.eof())
      ;
   return 0;
}
```

```cpp
istream& readparm(istream& s,int noparms,PARM *p)
// This streams extraction operator takes input from network definition file
// for one definition parameter. It reads in the name of the parameter
// and then looks up which entry in the parameter table to instantiate
// with a value.
{
    char keyword[NAMELEN],val[16];
    s >> keyword;
    if(!s || s.eof() || s.fail())  // end of file or failure to read keyword
        return s;

    for(int i=0;i<noparms;i++)
        if(!stricmp(keyword,p[i].name))
            break;

    if(i < noparms) // recognized parameter
        switch(p[i].type){
            case string:   s >> p[i].val.s; break;
            case integer:  s >> p[i].val.i; break;
            case real:     s >> p[i].val.f; break;
        }
    else
        s >> val;

    return s;
}

                typedef struct {
                    char name[16];
                    vartype type;
                    union {
                        char s[8];
                        float f
                        int i;
                    }val
                } PARM;
                istream& readparm(istream& s,
                                  int noparms,
                                  PARM *p);
                int readparms(int n, PARM *p,
                              char *name);
```

```
/////////////////////////////////////////////////////////
//                 NET CLASS
//
class net {
protected:
        char *name;  // string used as basename for files
        int n; // size of input layer
        int p; // size of output layer
        // learning rate (defined as 1 where not gradual)
        float learnrate;
        // decay (default constructed zero if not applicable)
        float decayrate;
        int iters;
        int cycleno;

        // private methods, since we don't know topology
        // they must be pure virtual
        virtual int saveweights() = 0;
        virtual int loadweights() = 0;
        int skipcmt(ifstream& s);
public:
        enum parmtype {inputs,outputs,learn,decay};
        net(){};
        net(char *s);
        net(char *s,int noparms,parm *p);
        ~net();

        // encode and recall and "pure virtual" which makes
        // the net class abstract
        virtual int encode(vecpair& v) = 0;
        virtual vec recall(vec& v) = 0;
        virtual float cycle(ifstream& s);
        virtual void train();
        int getiters (void) {return iters;}
        // floating point value indicates percentage correct of test
        virtual float test();
        virtual void run();
};
```

I.3.2 NET.CPP

```
// NET.CPP
// Source code for abstract neural network base class

#include "net.hpp"

/////////////////////////////////////////////////////////////////////
//                                                      NET CLASS
// Abstract neural net class methods
net::net(char *s)
{
    char fn[16];
    name=new char[strlen(s)+1];
    strcpy(name,s);
    const NOPARMS=5;
    PARM parms[5]={
        {"INPUTS",   integer},
        {"OUTPUTS",  integer},
        {"RATE",     real},
        {"DECAY",    real},
        {"ITERS",    integer}
    };
    readparms(NOPARMS,parms,name);
    n = parms[0].val.i;
    p = parms[1].val.i;
    learnrate = parms[2].val.f;
    decayrate = parms[3].val.f;
    iters = parms[4].val.i;
    return;
}


void net::train()
{
        if stream *s; < float ret;
        if(loadweights())
                cout << "Training from stored weights.\n";
        char fn[_MAX_PATH];
        sprintf(fn,"%s.FCT",name);
        cout << "Training from " << fn << ".  Press any key to stop.\n";
```

```
        for(;;){
                s=new ifstream(fn,ios::in);

                if(!*s){
                        cout << "Failed to open fact file.\n";
                        return 0;
                }
                cout << "Cycle " << ++cycleno << ": ";
                ret=cycle(*s);
                delete s;


                if(ret>=1.0 || kbhit()){
                        cout << "Training suspended at " << cycleno
                                << " cycles.\n";
                        break;

                }
        }

        saveweights();

}


float net::cycle(ifstream& s)
{
        vecpair v(n,p);
        float good,total;

        skipcmt(s);
        for(;;){
                s >> v;

                if(s.eof()||s.fail())break;
                v.scale(*minvecs,*maxvecs);
                if(encode(v))
                        good++;
                total++;
                if(kbhit()){return 1.0;}
        }

        return good/total;
}
```

```
int net::skipcmt(ifstream& inf)
{
        int c;
        inf.unsetf(inf.skipws);
        if(inf.peek()==':'){
                do{
                        c=inf.get();
                        if(c<0)
                                return 0;
                } while( (c!=0xd) && (c!=0xa) );
                inf.setf(inf.skipws);
                return 1;
        }

        else{
                inf.setf(inf.skipws);
                return 0;
        }
}
```

■ I.4 BACKPROPAGATION

I.4.1 BP.HPP

```
// BP.HPP
// Header file for backprop implementation
// Copyright (c) 1990, Adam Blum

#include "net.hpp"


class bp: public net {   // backpropagation network derived from
private:
        int q;  // size of hidden layer
        matrix *W1,*W2;   // synapse weight matrices
        matrix *dW1,*dW2;  // used to compute changes to matrices
        vec *h,*o,*d,*e,*thresh1,*thresh2;
```

```
        int epoch;
        vec *totd,*tote;
        vecpair *minvecs,*maxvecs;
        float momentum,initrange;

        // private member functions
        // these are helper member functions
        void initvals(matrix& m,const vec& v1,const vec& v2,
                      const float rate=1.0,const float momentum=0.0);
        int bp::saveweights();
        int bp::loadweights();
        float bp::cycle(istream& s);
public:
        // public member functions
        bp(char *s);              // constructs based on <name>.DEF file
        ~bp();                    // destructor
        // override pure virtual functions
        int encode(vecpair& v); // store one pattern pair
        // recall an output pattern given an input
        vec recall(vec& v);
};
```

1.4.2 BP.CPP

```
// BP.CPP
// Implementation of backprop net
// Copyright (c) 1990,91, Adam Blum

#include "bp.hpp"

extern int trace;

bp::bp(char *s):net(s) // constructor
{
    const NOPARMS = 5;
```

```
PARM parms[NOPARMS]={
    {"HIDDEN",    integer},
    {"MOMENTUM",  real},
    {"INITRANGE", real},
    {"EPOCH",     integer},
    {"TOLERANCE", real}
};
readparms(NOPARMS,parms,name);
q   = parms[0].val.i;
momentum = parms[1].val.f;
initrange = parms[2].val.f;
epoch    = parms[3].val.i;
tolerance = parms[4].val.f;

// initialize both weight matrices to random values from -1 to +1

W1=new matrix(n,q,-initrange);
W2=new matrix(q,p,-initrange);

dW1=new matrix(n,q);
dW2=new matrix(q,p);
h=new vec(q);
o=new vec(p);
d=new vec(p);
e=new vec(q);

thresh1=new vec(q);
thresh1->randomize(initrange);
thresh2=new vec(p);
thresh2->randomize(initrange);

if(epoch){
    totd=new vec(p);
    tote=new vec(q);
}

minvecs=new vecpair(n,q);
maxvecs=new vecpair(n,q);

cycleno=0;
}
```

```
bp::~bp()
{
        delete W1;
        delete W2;

        delete dW1;
        delete dW2;

        delete h;
        delete o;
        delete d;
        delete e;

        if(epoch){
                delete totd;
                delete tote;
        }

        delete minvecs;
        delete maxvecs;
}


//////////////////////////////////////////////////
//
// BACKPROP ALGORITHM METHODS - ENCODE AND RECALL
//

int bp::encode(vecpair& v)
{
        float maxd:ff;
        // Step 1) from text: h=F(W1 i)
        *h = (*W1) * (*(v.a));
        // get vector that is dot-product of input and weight matrix
        // apply sigmoid activation function to result
        h->sigmoid(*thresh1);

        // Step 2) from text: o=F(W2 h)
        *o=(*W2)*(*h);

        if(trace){
                cout << "Unsquashed guess: " << *o;
        }
```

```
o->sigmoid(*thresh2);

if (epoch){// adjust weights at the end of the cycle

        // Step 3 from text: d = o (1-o) (o-t)
        // the somewhat circuitous code is
        // so that we can use existing
        // overloaded operators from the vector class
        *d = (*(v.b) - *o);

        if(trace){
                cout.precision(2);
                cout << "\nOutput: " << *(v.b) << " Guess: " << *o;
        }
        float maxdiff=d->maxval();
        *d  = *d * o->d_logistic();

        // Step 4 from text: e = b (1-b) W2 d
        *e = ((*W2) * *d) *        // matrix x vector = vector
                // returns dot-product of vec & complement
                h->d_logistic();

        // weights will be adjusted at end of cycle with
        // following totals

        *totd += *d;

        *tote += *e;


}       // pattern-by-pattern training
else{
        // Step 3 from text: d = o (1-o) (o-t)
        // the somewhat secuitous code is so that we
        // can use existing
        // overloaded operators from the vector class

        *d = (*(v.b) - *o);

        cout.precision(2);
```

```
            if(trace)
                    cout << "\nOutput: " << *(v.b) << " Guess: " << *o;

        float maxdiff=d->maxval();
        *d   = *d * o->d_logistic();

        // Step 4 from text: e = b (1-b) W2 d
        *e = ((*W2) * *d) *        // matrix x vector = vector
                    // returns dot-product of vec & complement
                    h->d_logistic();

        // Step 5: W2 = W2 + α h d + Θ W2(i-1)
        // " α  h  d " part
        initvals(*dW2,(*h),*d,learnrate,momentum);
        (*W2) += *dW2;

        *thresh2 += ( (*d) * learnrate );

        // Step 6: W1 = W1 + α i e + Θ W2(i-1)
        initvals(*dW1,*(v.a),*e,learnrate,momentum);
        (*W1) += *dW1;

        *thresh1 += ( (*e) * learnrate);


    }

    if(maxdiff < tolerance ){
            return 1;
    }
    else {
            return 0;
    }
}


void bp::initvals(matrix& m,const vec& v1,const vec& v2,
                const float rate,const float momentum)
// Used to initialize a matrix to the vector product
// of v1 and v2 times the learn rate
// also adding in the previous contents of the matrix
// multiplied by a momentum term.
```

```
        {
                for(int  i=0;i<m.depth();i++)
                        for(int  j=0;j<m.width();j++)
                        m.setval(i,j,(m.getval (i,j) *momentum)
                                + (v1.v[i]*V2.V[j])*rate);
        }


vec bp::recall(vec& v)
{
        // Step 1:  h = F(W1 i)
        // get vector that is dot-product of input and weight matrix
        // apply sigmoid activation function to result
        *h=(*W1)*v;
        h->sigmoid(*thresh1);

        // Step 2:  o = F (W2 h)
        vec out(this->p);
        out=(*W2)*(*h);
        out.sigmoid(*thresh2);

        return out;
}


//
// This will get called from the neural network train since train
// will call the most derived cycle method.
// We need to override the network cycle since backpropagation
// may require the weights to be updated at the end of a cycle.

float bp::cycle(ifstream& s)
{
        vecpair v(n,p);
        float good,total;

        s >> *minvecs;

        s >> *maxvecs;
```

```
      skipcmt(s);
      for(;;){
              s >> v;


              if(s.eof()||s.fail())break;
              v.scale(*minvecs,*maxvecs);
              if(encode(v)){
                      good++;
                      if(!trace)
                              cout << '.';
              }
              else
                      if(!trace)
                              cout << 'x';
              total++;
              if(kbhit()){return 1.0;}
      }
      if(epoch){ // adjust weights at end of cycle
              // W2 = W2 + α  h d (total)
              dW2->initvals((*h),*totd,learnrate); // " α  h d " part
              (*W2) += *dW2;

              *thresh2 += ( (*totd) * learnrate )

              // W1 = W1 + α i e (total)
              dW1->initvals(*(v.a),*tote,learnrate);
              (*W1) +=  *dW1;

              *thresh1 += ( (*tote) * learnrate );

      }

  cout << "\n" << good/total * 100 << " percent correct.\n";
  return good/total;
}


              total++;
      }
  cout << good/total << " percent correct. \n";
  return good/total
}
```

```
//////////////////////////////////////////////
//
//          BACKPROP LEVEL INPUT/OUTPUT METHODS:
//          Saving and loading weights, skipping comments.
//

int bp::saveweights()
{
    FILE *f;
    char fn[32];

    sprintf(fn,"%s.WTS",name);
    f=fopen(fn,"wb");

    if(f <= 0)  // couldn't open the file
        // save failed!
        return 0;

    fwrite(&cycleno,sizeof(int),1,f);

    if(!(W1->save(f))
        || !(W2->save(f))
        || !(thresh1->save(f))
        || !(thresh2->save(f))
      )
    {
        fclose(f);
        return 0;
    }
    else
        fclose(f);
    /* put matrices into ".MAT" in readable form */

    if(trace){
        sprintf(fn,"%s.MAT",name);
        ofstream matf(fn,ios::out);
        matf << "First matrix contains: \n"
            << *W1
            << "Second matrix contains: \n"
      << *W2;
    }
    return 1;
}
```

```
int bp::loadweights()
{
   FILE *f;
   char fn[32];
   sprintf(fn,"%s.WTS",name);
   f=fopen(fn,"rb");
   if(f<=0) // couldn't open file
      return 0;
   fread(&cycleno,sizeof(int),1,f);
   if(    !(W1->load(f))
      || !(W2->load(f))
      || !(thresh1->load(f))
      || !(thresh2->load(f))
     )
   {
      fclose(f);
      return 0;
   }
   else
      fclose(f);
   return 1;
}
```

∎ I.5 COUNTERPROPAGATION

I.5.1 CPN.HPP

```
// CPN.HPP
// Include for Counterpropagation Network Implementation

// include vec and matrix classes
#include "net.hpp"
```

```
class layer: public matrix, public net {
public:
        void chgwts_koh(int c,vec& input);
        void chgwts_gross(int r,double activation,vec& output);
        layer(int n,int p,double randlimit,double r,double d):
                matrix(n,p,randlimit){learnrate=r;decay=d;}
        ~layer(){};
};

class cpn: public net {
protected:
        int q;
        layer *koh;
        layer *gross;
        double noise;
        double range;
        int *wins;        // keep track of wins for each Kohonen neuron
        double scaling;
        int winners;

public:
        cpn(char *s);
        ~cpn(){};
        void encode(const vecpair& AC);
        vec recall(vec& A);

}; // network layer class
```

I.5.2 CPN.CPP

```
// CPN.CPP
// Implementation of Hecht-Nielsen's counterpropagation network model
// Using Turbo C++ 1.0
// Copyright (c) 1990, Adam Blum

#include "cpn.hpp"
extern int trace;
```

```
void layer::chgwts_koh(int r,vec& input)
{
        vec v=rowslice(r);
        vec w=input-v;
        v+=(w*learnrate);
        learnrate/=2; // learn rate decay
        insertrow(v,r);
}

void layer::chgwts_gross(int c,double activation,vec& output)
{
        // grab the c-th weight vector column out of the matrix
        vec v=colslice(c);
        v*=(1-decay rate);                           // decay it
        // now compute the correlation vector
        // (output vector x hidden level activation)
        // scale this correlation vector by learn rate
        // add it to weight vector
        vec tmp=(output*activation);
        tmp*=learnrate;
        v+=tmp;
//      if(trace)
//              cout << "New Grossberg layer column "
//              << c << ": " << v << "\n";
        insertcol(v,c);                      // reinsert into matrix
}


cpn::cpn(char *s):net(s)
{
        const NOPARMS=5;
   PARM  parms[NOPARMS]={
      {"HIDDEN",integer},
      {"RANGE",real},
      {"NOISE",real},
      {"SCALING",real},
      {"WINNERS",integer}
   };
   readparms(NOPARMS,parms,name);
   q = parms[0].val.i;
   range = parms[1].val.f;
```

```
noise = parms[2].val.f;
scaling = parms[3].val.f;
winners = parms[4].val.i;
   /* Kohonen layer is initialized to random value
       between 0 and 1 */
   koh=new layer(p,n,range,learnrate,0);
      wins=new int[p]; // counter to keep track of wins
                      //for each Kohonen neuron
   for(int i=0;i<p;i++)
     wins[i]=0;
   cycle=0;
   /* Grossberg layer of CPN has decay term,
     but is initialized to 0 */
     gross=new layer(q,p,0,learnrate,decay);
}



void cpn::encode(const vecpair& AC)
{
        double hidactivation;
        (AC.a)->garble(noise); // add random noise to pattern
        AC.a->normalizeon();
        if(trace)
               cout << "Normalized input vector " << *(AC.a);
        int g;
        g=koh->closestrow(*(AC.a),wins,scaling);
        wins[(int)g]++;
        if(trace){
               cout << "Winning Kohonen node: " << g
                      << " (" << wins[g] << "-th win)\n";
               cout << " (output vector) " << *(AC.b) << "\n";
        }
        // (*(AC.a))*=(++cycle/(wins[g]+1));
        koh->chgwts_koh(g,*(AC.a));
        hidactivation=(koh->rowslice(g)*(*(AC.a)));
        gross->chgwts_gross(g,hidactivation,*(AC.b));

}
```

```
vec cpn::recall(vec& A)
{
        A.normalizeon();
#if MAXACTIV
        vec b=(*koh)*A; //* n-by-p matrix * n-length vector =
                        //p-length vector */
        int g=b.maxindex();
#else
        int g=koh->closestrow(A,wins,scaling);
#endif

        if(trace)
                cout << "Chose column " << g << "\n";
        return (gross->colslice(g)); /* g-th q-length vector */
}
```

■ 1.6 BAM SYSTEMS

1.6.1 BAM.HPP

```
////////////////////////////////////////////////////////////
// BAM.HPP
// Provide vector, matrix, vector pair, matrix, BAM matrix, and BAM
// System classes and methods to implement BAM System concept.
//
// Extended note:
// This is an implementation of the concept of bidirectional
// associative memories as developed by Bart Kosko and others.
// It includes the extended concept introduced by Patrick Simpson
// of the "BAM System." Where reasonable Simpson's notation has
// been maintained. The presentation benefits greatly from C++ and OOP,
// (in that) it is both easier to understand than a "pseudocode"
// [version,] yet more precise (in that it works!)
//
// Developed with the Zortech C++ compiler, Version 2.0
// Copyright (c) Adam Blum, 1989,90,91
```

```
#include<stdlib.h>
#include<io.h>
#include<stdio.h>
#include<string.h>
#include<limits.h>
#include<ctype.h>

#include "net.hpp"

#include "debug.h" // debugging devices
#ifdef _ZTC_
#define max(a,b)         (((a) > (b)) ? (a) : (b))
#define min(a,b)         (((a) < (b)) ? (a) : (b))
#endif

const MAXMATS=10; // maximum number of matrices in BAM System

class bam_matrix: public matrix {

        private:

                int K; // number of patterns stored in matrix
                vecpair *C; // actual pattern pairs stored
                int feedthru(vec& A,vec& B);
                int sigmoid(int n); // sigmoid threshold function

        public:

                bam_matrix(int n=ROWS,int p=COLS);
                ~bam_matrix();
                // but we supply it with the actual matrix A|B
                void encode(const vecpair& AB); // self-ref version
                // uncode only necessary for BAM-System
                void uncode(const vecpair& AB); // self-ref version
                vecpair recall(const vec& A);
                int check();
                int check(const vecpair& AB);
                // Lyapunov energy function: E=-AWBtranspose
                int energy(const matrix& m1);
}; // BAM matrix
```

```
class bam_system: public net {
                bam_matrix *W[MAXMATS];
                int M;  // number of matrices
                int saveweights(void);
                int loadweights(void);
        public:

                bam_system(char *s,int rows,int cols,int nomats=1);
                bam_system(char *s,int nomats=1);
                // construct from .DEF
                ~bam_system();
                void encode(vecpair& AB);
                vecpair recall pair(vec& A);
                friend ostream& operator<<(ostream& s,bam_system& b);
};  // BAM system class
```

1.6.2 BAM.CPP

```
/////////////////////////////////////
// BAM.CPP
// Provide vector, matrix, vector pair, matrix, BAM matrix,
// and BAM System classes to implement BAM Systems
//
// Extended note:
// This is an implementation of the concept of bidirectional
// associative memories as developed by Bart Kosko and others.
// It includes the extended concept introduced by Patrick Simpson
// of the "BAM System." Where reasonable Simpson's notation has
// been maintained. The presentation benefits greatly from C++ and OOP,
// (in that) it is both easier to understand than a "pseudocode" version,
// yet more precise (in that it works!)
//
// Developed with the Zortech C++ compiler, Version 2.0
// Copyright (c) 1989,90,91 Adam Blum


#include"bam.hpp"
```

```
//////////////////////////////////
//bam_matrix   member functions

bam_matrix::bam_matrix(int n,int p):matrix(n,p)
{         // the maximum number of pattern pairs storable
          // is around min(n,p) where n and p are
          // the dimensions of the matrix
        C=new vecpair[min(n,p)*2];
        K=0;
}
bam_matrix::~bam_matrix()
{
} // destructor

void bam_matrix::encode(const vecpair& AB)

// encode a pattern pair
{
        //D(cout << "BAM Matrix encoding: " << AB;)
        matrix T=AB;
        (*this)+=T; // add the matrix transpose to the current matrix
        C[K]=AB;
        K++;
}

void bam_matrix::uncode(const vecpair& AB)
// get rid of a stored pattern (by encoding A-B complement)
{
        D(cout << "uncode\n";)
        vec v=*(AB.b)*-1;
        matrix T(*(AB.a),v); // T is A transpose B complement
        *this+=T;// add the matrix transpose to the current matrix
        K--;
}

vecpair bam_matrix::recall(vec& A)
// BAM Matrix recall algorithm (used by BAM SYSTEM recall)
{
                vec C=A;
        int givenrow=(C.length()==width());
        D(cout<<"BAM matrix recall of" << C <<
            (givenrow?"(row)\n":"(col)\n");)
```

```
            vec B(givenrow?depth():width(),1);
            for(;;){
            // feed vectors through matrix until "resonant" pattern-pair
                    feedthru(C,B);
                    // stop when returned A = input A
                    if(feedthru(B,C))break;
            }
            D(cout<< "resonant pair " << C << "\n and " << B << "\n";)
            if(givenrow)
                    return vecpair(B,C);
            else
                    return vecpair(C,B);
}
int bam_matrix::feedthru(vec& A,vec& B)
{
        //D(cout << "Feeding " << A << "\n";  )

        vec temp=B; int n;
        for(int i=0;i<B.length();i++){
                if(A.length()==width())
                        n=sigmoid(A*rowslice(i));
                else
                        n=sigmoid(A*colslice(i));
                if(n)
                        B.set(i,n);
        }
        return B==temp;
}


int bam_matrix::sigmoid(int n)
// VERY simple (but classic one for BAM) threshold function
//
//
//              1 --------------
//                 |
//   - -----------             +
//              -1
{
        if(n<0)return -1;
        if(n>0)return 1;
        return 0;
}
```

```
int bam_matrix::check()
// check to see if we have successfully encoded pattern pair
{
        D(cout << "Check BAM matrix for " << K << " pattern pairs\n"; )
        vecpair AB(depth(),width());
        for(int i=0; i<K; i++){
                AB=recall(*(C[i].a));
                if(!(AB==C[i])){
                        D(cout <<"failed check\n "; )
                        return 0;

                }
        }
        D(cout << "passed check\n "; )
        return 1;

}

int bam_matrix::check(const vecpair& AB)
{
        // different check routine for orthogonal construction BAM
        //check to see energy of present pattern pair to matrix
        // is equal to orthogonal BAM energy
        matrix T(AB);
        return energy(T)== -depth()*width();

}

int bam_matrix::energy(const matrix& m1)
{
        int sum=0,rows=min(depth(),m1.depth()),
        cols=min(width(),m1.width());
        for(int i=0; i<rows; i++)
                for(int j=0; j<cols; j++)
                        sum+=(m1.getval(i,j)*this->m[i][j]);
        D(cout << "Energy of matrix " << -sum << "\n"; )
        return -sum;

}

///////////////////////////////////////////
// bam system  functions
// top level of system (for now)

// constructor

// construct from configuration (.DEF file)
```

```
bam_system::bam_system(char *s):net(s)
{
    PARM parms[3]={
      {"NOMATS",integer},
      {"INPUTS",integer},
      {"OUTPUTS",integer}
      };
    readparms(3,parms,name);
    M = parms[0].val.i;
    n = parms[1].val.i;
    p = parms[2].val.i;

    for(int i=0;i<M;i++)
       W[i]=new bam_matrix(n,p);
}


// construct from explicit parameters
bam_system::bam_system(char *s,int rows,int cols,int nomats)
{
        name=new char[strlen(s)+1];
        strcpy(name,s);
        n=rows;
        p=cols;
        M=nomats;
        for(int i=0;i<M;i++)
                W[i]=new bam_matrix(n,p);
}


bam_system::~bam_system() // destructor
{
        delete name;
        for(int i=0;i<M;i++)
                delete W[i];
}
int bam_system::saveweights(void){return 1;}
int bam_system::loadweights(void){return 1;}

void bam_system::encode(vecpair& AB)
// encode the pattern pair AB into the BAM system
{
        D(cout << "BAM System encode\n";)
```

```
              for(int h=0;h<M;h++){
                        W[h]->encode(AB);
                        if(!W[h]->check())
                                W[h]->uncode(AB);
                        else
                                break;
              }
              if(h==M){ // all matrices full, add another
                        D(cout << "Allocating new matrix.\n"; )
                        if(h<MAXMATS){
                                W[M]=new bam_matrix(n,p);
                                if(!W[M]){
                                  cout << "Failed to allocate new matrix.\n";
                                  exit(1);
                                }
                                else {
                                        W[M]->encode(AB);
                                        M++;
                                }
                        }
                        else{

                                cout << "BAM System full\n";
                                exit(1);
                        }
                }
}
vecpair bam_system::recall pair (vec& A)
// presented with pattern A, recall pair will return pattern-PAIR
{
    int req_E;
    matrix *M1,*M2;
    vecpair tempv(W[0]->width(),W[0]->depth(),1),
            bestv(W[0]->width(),W[0]->depth(),1);
     int E,emin=INT_MAX;
     D(cout << "BAM System recall\n"; )
     for(int h=0;h<M;h++){
         tempv=W[h]->recall(A);
         D(cout << h <<"-th matrix, returned vecpair "<< tempv; )
         M1=new matrix(tempv);
         if(!M1)
             cout << "Failed to create matrix.\n" ;
```

```
            E=W[h]->energy(*M1);
            D(cout << "computed energy" << E; )
            if(A.length()==W[h]->width())
                    M2=new matrix(*(tempv.a),A);
            else
              M2=new matrix(A,*(tempv.b));
            req_E=W[h]->energy(*M2);
            D(cout << "required energy" <<req_E; )
            if (   abs( E-(-(W[h]->depth()*W[h]->width()))) < emin )
                && ( E == req_E        )
            )
            {

                    emin=abs(E-(W[h]->depth()*W[h]->width()));
                    bestv=tempv;

            }
            delete M1;
            delete M2;
        }
      cout << "recall return " << bestv;
      return bestv;
}
vec bam_system::recall(vec& A)
{
    vec out;
    vecpair vp;
    vp=recallpair(A);
    if ( A.length() == vp.a->length() ) {
        A = *(vp.a);
        out=*(vp.b);
    }
    else {
        out=*(vp.a);
        A = *(vp.b);
    }
    return out;
}
ostream& operator<<(ostream& s,bam_system& b)
// operator to print out contents of entire BAM System
{
        for(int i=0;i<b.M;i++)
                s<< "BAM Matrix " << i << ": \n" << *(b.W[i]) << "\n";
        return s;
}
```

■ I.7 HOPFIELD NETS

I.7.1 HOP.HPP

```
// HOP.HPP
// Implementation of Hopfield-Tank model

// include character vec and matrix classes
#include "net.hpp"



class hop {
        double initrange;
        int saveweights(void);
        int loadweights(void);

public:
        hop(char *s);
        ~hop(){};
        int encode(const vec& A);
        int encode(vecpair& A);
        vec recall(vec& A);
        int feedthru(vec& A);
};
```

1.7.2 HOP.CPP

```cpp
// HOP.CPP
// Implementation of Hopfield-Tank model
// Copyright (c) 1990, Adam Blum

#include "hop.hpp"
hop::hop(char *s):net(s)
{
    const NOPARMS=1;
    PARM parms[NOPARMS]={
        {"INITRANGE",real},
    };
    readparms(NOPARMS,parms,s);
    initrange=parms[0].val.f;
}

int hop::encode(vec& A)
{
    double delta;
    for (int i=0;i<n;i++){
        for (int j=0;j<n;j++){
            delta = A[i]*A[j];
            m[i][j] += delta;
        }
    }
    return 1;
}

int hop::encode(vecpair& vp)
{
    encode(*(vp.a));
    return 1;
}
```

```
vec hop::recall(vec& A)
{
        for(;;){
                if(feedthru(A))break;
        }
        vec tmp=A;
        return tmp;
}

int hop::feedthru(vec& A)
{
    vec temp=A;double val;
    for(int i=0;i<n;i++){
        val = rowslice(i) * temp;
        val = logistic(val);
        if(val)
            A.set(i,val);
    }
    return A==temp;
}


int hop::saveweights(void){return 1;}
int hop::loadweights(void){return 1;}
```

APPENDIX II
LISTINGS FOR
APPLICATIONS

■ II.1 DJ30 STOCK PREDICTOR

II.1.1 Input Factors for DJ30 Stock Predictor

There are three input factors for each of the following stocks: one representing price change, one representing volatility range, and one representing volume.

AL	Aluminum Corp. of America	MMM	Minnesota Mining and Manufacturing
ALD	Allied-Signal	MO	Philip Morris
AXP	American Express	MRK	Merck
BA	Boeing	NAV	Navistar
BS	Bethlehem Steel	PA	Primerica
CHV	Chevron	PG	Proctor & Gamble
DD	DuPont	S	Sears
EK	Eastman Kodak	T	AT&T
GE	General Electric	TX	Texaco
GM	General Motors	UK	Union Carbide
GT	Goodyear	UTX	United Technologies
IBM	International Business Machines	X	USX
IP	International Paper	XON	Exxon
KO	Coca-Cola	WX	Westinghouse
MCD	McDonald's	Z	Woolworth

Other input factors are:

FFRT	Federal funds rate	SP500N	Standard & Poor's 500 stocks
PRMR	Prime rate	XVG	Value Line Composite
USTBA	U.S. Treasury bill yields—91-day bills	NYSEI	NYSE advances
USTBB	U.S. Treasury bill yields—182-day bills	NYSEJ	NYSE declines
		NYSEK	NYSE unchanged
XRGM	Exchange rate—German mark	NYSEL	NYSE volume
HRJY	Exchange rate—Japanese yen	NYSUP	NYSE advance volume
DJ30	Dow Jones Industrial Average	NYSDN	NYSE decline volume

II.1.2 DJ30 Predictor Definition File

```
INPUTS 106
HIDDEN 64
OUTPUTS 30
INITRANGE 0.3
RATE 0.2
DECAY 0.05
MOMENTUM 0.1
INITRANGE 0.3
TOLERANGE 0.1
EPOCH 0
```

■ II.2 IMAGECPN

This is the source code for the handwritten-digit recognizer. Our image recognizer is embodied in the class IMAGECPN. This is based on the counterpropagation network (the CPN class, presented in Appendix I).

It consists of three files. IMAGECPN.HPP is a header file containing the class definition for IMAGECPN and the class IMAGE. IMAGECPN.CPP contains the implementation of the class. TESTIMAG.CPP is a test program for the image recognizer, which runs on PCX files containing images of handwritten digits.

II.2.1 IMAGECPN.HPP

```
// IMAGECPN.HPP
// Counterpropagation network used to recognize handwritten digits
```

```
        #include "cpn.hpp"
        // Craig Lindley's PCX structure definitions
        extern "C" {
        #include "pcx.h"
        }

const PCXROWS=480;
const PCXCOLS=640;
const TRUE=1;
const FALSE=0;
class image:public matrix {
public:
        // constructor
        image(int rows,int cols):matrix(rows,cols,(float)0){}
        int readpcx(char *pcxname);
        void zoomout(image& i);
        void imagevec(vec *v);
};

class imagecpn: public cpn {
public:
        imagecpn(char *s):cpn(s){}
        ~imagecpn(){}
        void train();
        void run();
};

static ExpandScanLine (ifstream& s,
                PCXFile& PCXData,
                BYTE *ScanLine,
                BYTE *PixelColorNum,
                unsigned ImageWidth);
```

II.2.2 IMAGECPN.CPP

```
// IMAGECPN.CPP
//

#include "imagecpn.hpp"
```

```
void imagecpn::train()
{
        char fn[16],pcxfn[32],c;
        int i;
        vecpair imagepair(n,10);
        float scale=(float)n/(float)((long)PCXROWS*(long)PCXCOLS);
        image smallimg((int)((float)PCXROWS*scale),
                (int)((float)PCXCOLS*scale));
        image origimg(PCXROWS,PCXCOLS);

        sprintf(fn,"%s.FCT",name);

        ifstream fct(fn,ios::in);
        for(;;){
        // read the PCX file-digit name pair from file line
        for(i=0;
            ( (pcxfn[i]=fct.get())!=',') && !fct.eof() && !isspace(pcxfn[i])
            ;i++)
            ;
        pcxfn[i]=0;

        if( !fct || fct.eof() || !pcxfn[0] )
            break; // stop at end of file or error

        if(!smallimg.readpcx(pcxfn))
            break; // ... or if we can't open the .PCX file, or there was
                   // an error

        if(trace)
            cout << "Image matrix: " << smallimg;


        smallimg.imagevec(imagepair.a);

        // second part of pattern pair is the spelling of the word for the digit
        for(i=0; (c=fct.get())!= 0xa; i++)
            imagepair.b->set(i,(float)(c-'0'));

        encode(imagepair);
        }

}
```

```
void imagecpn::run()
{
   char fn[16],pcxfn[32],c;
   int i;
   vec invec(n),outvec(p);
   float scale= pow((float)n/(float)((long)PCXROWS*(long)PCXCOLS),0.5);
   image smallimg((int)((float)PCXROWS*scale),(int)((float)PCXCOLS*scale));

   sprintf(fn,"%s.IN",name);
   ifstream infile(fn,ios::in);

   sprintf(fn,"%s.OUT",name);
   ofstream outfile(fn,ios::out);

   for(;;){ // keep going until we run out of pattern pairs or a file
            // is not found

      if( !infile || infile.eof() )
         break; // stop at end of file or error

      // read the PCX file-digit name pair from file line
      for(i=0;
         ( (pcxfn[i]=infile.get())!=',') && !infile.eof() && !isspace(pcxfn[i])
         ; i++)
         ;
      pcxfn[i]=0;


      if(!pcxfn[0] || !smallimg.readpcx(pcxfn))
         break; // or if there are no more file names
                // ... or if we can't open the .PCX file, or there was
                // an error

      if(trace)
         cout << "Image matrix: " << smallimg;

      smallimg.imagevec(&invec);

      outvec=recall(invec);
```

```
        if(trace)
            cout << "Output vector: " << outvec;

        outfile << outvec << endl;

    }

}
void image::imagevec(vec *v)
{

    int j:
    for(int i=0;  i<depth();i++)
            for(j=0;j<width();j++)
                    v->set(i*width()+j,m[i][j]);
}


void image::zoomout(image& i)
{

    int row,col,x,y,sum;
    int yfactor=r/i.r;
    int xfactor=c/i.c;
    for(row=0;row<r;row++)
            for(col=0;col<c;col++){
                    sum=0;
                    for(y=0;y<yfactor;y++)
                            for(x=0;x<xfactor;x++)
                                    sum+=i.m[row*yfactor+y][row*xfactor+x];
                    m[row][col]=sum/(yfactor*xfactor);

            }

}


int image::readpcx(char *pcxname)
{

    PCXFile PCXData;
    unsigned ImageWidth, ImageHeight;
    BYTE ScanLine[MAXBYTESPERSCAN];
    BYTE PixelColorNum[MAXSCREENWIDTH];

    ifstream s(pcxname,ios::in|ios::binary);
    if (!s) {
            cerr << "Failed to open file.\n";
            return FALSE;
    }
```

```
        s.read((unsigned char *)&PCXData,sizeof(PCXData));
        if(PCXData.PCXHeader.Header != PCXHdrTag){
             cerr << "Not a PCX file.\n";
             return FALSE;
        }


    /*
    From the header information determine the size of the buffer
    required to store the image. Set the global vars ImageWidth
    and ImageHeight accordingly.
    */
    return TRUE;
    }



    if (PCXData.PCXHeader.X2 == 319)
    {
        ImageWidth  = 320;
        ImageHeight = 200;
    }
    else
    {
        ImageWidth = 640; ImageHeight = PCX Data.PCX Header.Vres;
    /* allocate far memory for the image */
    ImageMemory = (BYTE huge *) farcalloc((long) ImageWidth * ImageHeight,
                                        sizeof(BYTE));

    if (ImageMemory == NULL)
    {
       printf("Error Not enough memory for PCX buffer\n");
       return (ENoMemory);
    }


    /*
    Proceed to unpack and store the PCX data. A scan line at
    a time.
    */


    int x=0;
    for (int y=0; y < ImageHeight; y++)
    {
       if (ExpandScanLine(s,PCXData,ScanLine,PixelColorNum,ImageWidth)
```

```
        != TRUE)
        {
            printf("Error Scanline corrupt in PCX file\n");
            return FALSE;
        }
        PixelBufOffset = (long) y * ImageWidth;
        for (x=0; x < ImageWidth; x++)
        {
            ImageMemory[PixelBufOffset + x] =
                    PixelColorNum[x];
        }
    }

    /* "zoom out" the buffer to fit our available matrix */
    int yfactor = ImageHeight / r ;
    int xfactor = ImageWidth / c ;
    int row,col,sum,pixelval;

    /* sum the number of values to put them in the image */
    for(row=0; row<r; row++)
        for(col=0; col<c; col++){
            sum=0;
            /* add all values in [row,col] quadrant of full PCX image */
            for(y=0; y<yfactor; y++)
                for(x=0; x<xfactor; x++) {
                    pixelval= ImageMemory[(( (long)row * (long)yfactor + (long)y ) *
                    sum += pixelval ? 0 : 1;
                }
            m[row][col]  = sum ;
        }

    free(ImageMemory);
    }
return TRUE;
}


static ExpandScanLine (ifstream& s,
                                PCXFile& PCXData,
                                BYTE *ScanLine,
                                BYTE *PixelColorNum,
                                unsigned ImageWidth)
```

```
{
    register short      BitNum;
    register unsigned   ByteNum;
    register short      CharRead;
    unsigned            InPtr, RepCount, PixelsData;
    unsigned            BytesToRead, PlaneNum, ShiftCount;
    unsigned            ByteOffset, BitOffset;


    BytesToRead = PCXData.Info.NumOfPlanes * PCXData.Info.BytesPerLine;

    InPtr = ShiftCount = 0;                 /* initialize vars */
    do
    {
        CharRead = s.get();             /* read a byte from the file */
        if (CharRead == EOF)                /* error should never read EOF */
            return(FALSE);                  /* abort picture */

        if ((CharRead & 0xC0) == 0xC0)  /* a repeat tag ? */
        {
            RepCount = CharRead & ~0xC0;   /* repeat 1..63 */
            CharRead = s.get();         /* read byte to repeat */
            if (CharRead == EOF)            /* error should never read EOF */

                return(FALSE);              /* abort picture */

            while (RepCount--)              /* expand byte */
                ScanLine[InPtr++] =         /* RepCount times */
                    CharRead;
        }

        else                                /* just a byte of data */

        ScanLine[InPtr++] = CharRead;   /* store in buffer */
    } while (InPtr < BytesToRead);          /* expand a full scan line */

    if (PCXData.PCXHeader.X2 == 319)        /* if 256 color image */
        memcpy(PixelColorNum, ScanLine, ImageWidth);

    else                                    /* normal image file */
```

```
{
    /* clear PixelColorNum array to zeros */
    memset(PixelColorNum,'\0',ImageWidth);

    for (PlaneNum=0; PlaneNum < PCXData.Info.NumOfPlanes; PlaneNum++)
    {
      ByteOffset = PlaneNum * PCXData.Info.BytesPerLine;
      for (ByteNum=0; ByteNum < PCXData.Info.BytesPerLine; ByteNum++)
      {
          /* read 8 bits of pixel data for one plane */
          PixelsData = ScanLine[ByteOffset+ByteNum];
          BitOffset = ByteNum * BITSPERBYTE;

          for (BitNum=BITSPERBYTE-1; BitNum >= 0; BitNum--)
          {
              if (PixelsData & (1 << BitNum))
              {
                  /* OR in each component of the color */
                  PixelColorNum[BitOffset + (7 - BitNum)] |=
                    (1 << ShiftCount);
              }
          }
      }
      ShiftCount++;
    }
  }


/*
When we get here, the PixelColorNum array has a byte color value
for each pixel on the display. Return an indication that this operation
went smoothly.
*/


  return(TRUE);
}
```

II.2.3 TESTIMAG.CPP

```
/////////////////////////
// TESTCPN.CPP
// Interactive CPN System Demonstration Program
// Used to verify CPN system algorithms
// Developed with Borland C++ 2.0
// Copyright (c) 1990 Adam Blum

#define NDEBUG 1
#include"imagecpn.hpp"
char netname[16]="IMAGECPN"; // file where test data is stored
char *p;
int trace=0; // SET TRACE=<whatever> at DOS prompt to turn trace on
main(int argc,char **argv)
{
    trace=(p=getenv("TRACE"))?1:0;
    if(argc>1)
            strcpy(netname,argv[1]);
    imagecpn C(netname);
    for(int i=0;i<C.iters;i++)
            C.train();
    C.run();
}
```

■ II.3 SPELLBAM

II.3.1 SPELLBAM.HPP

```
///////////////////////////////////////////
// SPELLBAM.HPP
//
// Class for BAM System-based spelling checker
// Derive spelling checker from BAM System
// Copyright (c) 1991, Adam Blum
```

```cpp
#include"bam.hpp"


const NPC=5; // neurons per character, 2^5 = 32 (> 26)
const MAXSPELL=16;
const MAXPRONOUNCE=16;


class word { // spelling and pronunciation, needed by spellbam class
        friend ostream& operator<<(ostream& s,word& w);
        friend istream& operator>>(istream& s,word& w);
        char *spell;
        int splen;
        char *pronounce;
        int prlen;

public:

        word(int sp=MAXSPELL,int pr=MAXPRONOUNCE);
        ~word(){delete spell;delete pronounce;};
        void makevec(vecpair& v);
        void makeword(vecpair& v);
        int operator!();
        int spell_length();
        int pronounce_length();
        void input_spell();
};

class spellbam: public bam_system {
    int maxsplen;
    int maxprlen;
public:
    spellbam(char *s):bam_system(s){maxsplen=n/NPC;maxprlen=p/NPC;};
    ~spellbam(){}
    int encode_word(word& w);
    void recall_word(word& w);
    void train();
};
```

II.3.2 SPELLBAM.CPP

```
/////////////////////////////////////////////////
//                                    SPELLBAM.CPP
// Source code for member functions of SPELLBAM class


#include"spellbam.hpp"

int word::spell_length()
{
        return splen;
}

int word::pronounce_length()
{
        return prlen;
}

word::word(int sp,int pr)
{
        splen=sp;
        spell=new char[splen];
        prlen=pr;
        pronounce=new char[prlen];
}


void word::makevec(vecpair& v)
// convert the spelling and pronunciation strings
// to bit vectors
{
        for(int i=0;i<splen*NPC;i++)
                v.a->set(i, ((spell[i/NPC]-'@ ') & (0x01<<(i%NPC)))?1:-1);
        for(i=0;i<prlen*5;i++)
                v.b->set(i, ((pronounce[i/NPC]-'@ ') &
  (0x01<<(i%NPC)))?1:-1);
}

void word::makeword(vecpair& v)
```

```
// construct a word (spelling and pronunciation pair) from a vector pair
{
        int i,j;
        spell=new char[splen=v.a->length()/NPC];
        for(i=0;i<splen;i++){
                spell[i]='@ ';
                for(j=0;j<NPC;j++)
                        spell[i]+= (( ((*(v.a))[i*NPC+j]==1) ?1:0)
                                        * (0x01 << j));
                if(spell[i]=='@ '){
                        spell[i]=0;
                        break;
                }
        }
        pronounce=new char[prlen=v.b->length()/NPC];
        for(i=0;i<prlen;i++){
                pronounce[i]='@ ';
                for(j=0;j<NPC;j++)
                        pronounce[i]+=((((*(v.b))[i*NPC+j]==1) ?1:0)
                                        * (0x01 << j));
                if(pronounce[i]=='@ '){
                        pronounce[i]=0;
                        break;
                }
        }
}

int spellbam::encode_word(word& w)
{
        D(cout << "Encoding " << w; )
        vecpair v(n,p,-1);
        w.makevec(v);
        bam_system::encode(v); // BAM System encode
}

void spellbam::recall_word(word& w)
{
        vecpair v(n,p,-1);
        w.makevec(v);
        v=bam_system::recall(*(v.a));
        cout << "recalled " << v;
```

```
        w.makeword(v);
}

void spellbam::train()
{
        char fn[32];
        sprintf(fn,"%s.FCT",name);
        ifstream s(fn,ios::in);
        if(!s){
                D(cout << "Failed to open file.\n";)
        }
        else{
                D(cout << "Opened file.\n";)
                word w(maxsplen,maxprlen);
                for(;;){
                        s >> w;
                        if (s.eof() || !s || !w.spell_length
                        () || !w.pronounce_length())
                        break;
                        encode_word(w);
                        }
        D(cout << "Completed training from " << fn;)
        }
}

void word::input_spell()
{
        cin >> spell;
        splen=strlen(spell);
        prlen=0;
}

int word::operator!()
{
        if(!spell[0])
                return 1;
        return 0;
}

istream& operator>>(istream& s,word& w)
{
        int i=0;char skip[8];
```

```
        // get the spelling
        while((!(!s)&&!s.eof()) && (( w.spell[i++]=toupper(s.get()) )!=',')
            );
        if(!s||s.eof())
            return s;
        w.spell[i-1]=0;
        w.splen=i;
        // get the pronunciation
          i=0;
          while( (w.pronounce[i++]=toupper(s.get()))!=',');
          w.pronounce[i-1]=0;
          w.prlen=i;

          while(s.get()!='\n')
              ;
          return s;
}
ostream& operator<<(ostream& s,word& w)
{
        s       << "Spelled: " << w.spell
                << "\nPronounced: " << w.pronounce
                << "\n"
                ;
        return s;
}
```

II.3.3 TSTSPELL.CPP

```
////////////////////////////////////////////////////////////////////////
//                              TSTSPELL.CPP
//
// Interactive tester for SPELLBAM, BAM System-based spelling checker
//
// Usage: SPELLBAM <dictionary base name>
//                    Causes speller to be trained on specified
//                      .FCT file. Defaults to SPELLBAM.FCT.
```

```
#include "spellbam.hpp"

word w;
spellbam *speller;
char *p,name[9]="SPELLBAM";
int trace=0; // SET TRACE=<whatever> at DOS prompt to turn trace on


void main(int argc,char **argv)
{
     if(argc>1)
            strcpy(name,argv[1]);
     speller=new spellbam(name);
     cout << "Interactive BAM System Spell Checker Demonstration\n";
     trace=(p=getenv("TRACE"))?1:0;
     cout << "Training " << name << "\n";
     speller->train();
     cout<<"Enter words. Correct spelling and pronunciation
  will be recalled.\n"
     << "No word (just Enter) to end.\n\n" ;
     for(;;){
         cout << "Enter word: ";
         w.input_spell();
         if(!w)break;
         speller->recall(w);
         cout << "Recalled word and pronunciation\n" << w;
     }
}
```

∎ II.4 TRAVELING SALESMAN PROBLEM WITH HOPFIELD NET

```
// TSP.HPP
// Implementation of the Traveling Salesman Problem
// Using Hopfield net
#include "vecmat.hpp"
#include "math.h"
```

```cpp
#define MAXVEC 8
#define delt(x,y) (((x)==(y))?1:0)

class tsp: public hop {
    char name[9];
    int n;
    float W[MAXVEC][MAXVEC][MAXVEC][MAXVEC];
    matrix *d;
    double A,B,C,D;
    void setweights();
public:
    tsp(char *s);
    ~tsp(){};
    void run();
    matrix feed(matrix& M);
    double excitation(double net);
};


// TSP.CPP
// Source file containing methods for TSP class
// Implementation of solver for Traveling Salesman Problem
// Using Hopfield net

#include "tsp.hpp"

tsp::tsp(char *s):hop(s)
{
    char fn[32];
    const NOPARMS=6;
    PARM parms[NOPARMS]={
        {"NUMBER",integer},
        {"A",real},
        {"B",real},
        {"C",real},
        {"D",real},
        {"ITERS",integer}
    };
    strcpy(name,s);
    readparms(NOPARMS,parms,name);
    n = parms[0].val.i;
    A = parms[1].val.f;
```

```
    B = parms[2].val.f;
    C = parms[3].val.f;
    D = parms[4].val.f;
    iters = parms[5].val.i;
        sprintf(fn,"%s.DST",name);
        d=new matrix(n,n,fn);     // read in distance matrix
        setweights();
}


void tsp::setweights()
{
    int x,y,i,j;
    for(x=0;x<n;x++){
        for(y=0;y<n;y++){
            for(i=0;i<n;i++){
                for(j=0;j<n;j++){
                    W[x][y][i][j]=(float) (
                            -A*delt(x,y)*(1-delt(i,j))
                            -B*delt(i,j)*(1-delt(x,y))
                            -C
                            -( D
                               * d->getval(x,y)
                               * (delt(j,i+1)+delt(j,i-1)))
                                    )
                            ;
                }
            }
        }
    }
}

void tsp::run()
{
    int i;char fn[32];
    matrix m1(n,n,1,1);
    for(i=0;i<iters;i++)
            m1=feed(m1);
    sprintf(fn,"%s.OUT",name);
    ofstream out(fn,ios::out);
    out << m1;
}
```

```cpp
double step(double activation);


matrix tsp::feed(matrix& M)
{
    int x,y,i,j;
    double net;
    matrix tmp(n,n);
    for(x=0;x<n;x++){
            for(i=0;i<n;i++){
                net=0;
                for(y=0;y<n;y++)
                        for(j=0;j<n;j++)
                                net+=(M.getval(y,j)*W[x][i][y][j]);
                tmp.setval(x,i,excitation(net+(c*n)));
            }
    }
    return tmp;
}


double tsp::excitation(double input)
// this is the activation function used by Hopfield and Tank
{
    return atan(input);
}
char netname[16]="TSP";
int trace=0;
main(int argc,char **argv)
{
    trace=getenv("TRACE")?1:0;
    if(argc>1)
            strcpy(netname,argv[1]);
    tsp t(netname);
    t.run();
}
```

REFERENCES

■ NEURAL NETWORKS

[Anderson 90] Anderson, James, and Rosenfeld, David, eds., *Neurocomputing.* Cambridge, MA, The MIT Press, 1990.

[Eberhart 90] Eberhart, Russel C., and Dobbins, Roy W., *Neural Network PC Tools: A Practical Guide.* San Diego: Academic Press, 1990.

[Grossberg 82] Grossberg, Stephen, *The Adaptive Brain.* Vols. I and II. Boston: Reidel Press, 1982.

[Hebb 49] Hebb, Donald, *Organization of Behavior.* New York: John Wiley & Sons, 1949.

[Hecht-Nielsen 87] Hecht-Nielsen, Robert, "Counterpropagation networks," *Proceedings of the IEEE First International Conference on Neural Networks.* 1987.

[Hopfield 85] Hopfield, John, and Tank, David, "Neural computation of decisions in optimization problems," *Biological Cybernetics 52.*

[IJCNN 90] *Proceedings of the International Joint Conference on Neural Networks,* January 1990.

[Khanna 90] Khanna, T., *Foundations of Neural Networks.* Reading, MA: Addison-Wesley, 1990.

[Kohonen 84] Kohonen, T., *Self-Organization and Associative Memory,* 2nd ed. Berlin: Springer-Verlag, 1984.

[Kosko 88] Kosko, B., "Bidirectional associative memories," *IEEE Trans. Systems, Man, Cybernetics* SMC-L8, 49–60, January/February 1988.

[McCulloch 43] McCulloch, Warren, and Pitts, Walter, "A logical calculus of the ideas immanent in nervous activity," *Bulletin of Mathematical Biophysics,* 7.

[Mead 89] Mead, C., *Analog VLSI and Neural Systems.* Reading, MA: Addison-Wesley, 1989.

[Minsky 69] Minsky, Marvin, *Perceptrons.* 1969.

[Pao 89] Pao, Y., *Adaptive Pattern Recognition and Neural Networks.* Reading, MA: Addison-Wesley, 1989.

[Parker 82] Parker, "Lemma Logic." Paper, Stanford University, 1982.

[Rosenblatt 57] Rosenblatt, Frank, *The Perceptron: A Perceiving and Recognizing Automaton.* Cornell Aeronautical Laboratory, 1957.

[Rumelhart, Hinton 86] Rumelhart, David E., Hinton, Geoffrey, and Williams, Ronald J., "Learning representations by backpropagating errors," *Nature,* 323.

[Rumelhart 86] Rumelhart, David E., and McClelland, James L., eds., *Parallel Distributed Processing,* vols. I and II. Cambridge, MA: The MIT Press, 1986.

[Rumelhart 89] Rumelhart, David E., and McClelland, James L., eds., *Explorations in Parallel Distributed Processing,* Cambridge, MA: The MIT Press, 1989.

[Simpson 90b] Simpson, Patrick K., "Associative memory systems," *Proceedings of the International Joint Conference on Neural Networks,* January 1990.

[Simpson 90a] Simpson, Patrick K., *Artificial Neural Systems.* Elmsford, NY: Pergamon Press, 1990.

[Wasserman 90] Wasserman, Philip D., *Neurocomputing: Theory and Practice.* New York: Van Nostrand Reinhold, 1990.

[Wechsler 91] Wechsler, Harry, *Neural Networks for Perception, Vol. II: Computation, Learning, and Architectures.* San Diego: Academic Press, 1991.

[Werbos 74] Werbos, Paul. "Beyond regression: New tools for prediction and analysis in the behavioral sciences," Ph.D dis., Harvard University, 1974.

■ C++ AND OBJECT-ORIENTED PROGRAMMING

[ATT 90] AT&T, *AT&T C++ Language System Release 2.0 Product Reference Manual,* AT&T, 1989.

[Coad 91] Coad, Peter, and Yourdon, Ed, *Object-Oriented Design.* New York: Yourdon Press, 1991.

[Dewhurst 89] Dewhurst, Stephen C. and Stark, Kathy T., *Programming in C++.* New York: Prentice-Hall, 1989.

[Eckel 89] Eckel, Bruce, *Using C++*. New York: Osborne/McGraw-Hill, 1989.

[Ellis 90] Ellis, M. A., and Stroustrup, B. J., *The Annotated C++ Reference Manual*. Reading, MA: Addison-Wesley, 1990.

[Gorlen 90] Gorlen, Keith. New York: Wiley, 1990.

[Lippman 91] Lippman, S. B., *C++ Primer, 2nd ed.* Reading, MA: Addison-Wesley, 1991.

[Meyer 89] Meyer, Bertrand E., *Object-Oriented Software Contruction*. Reading, MA: Addison-Wesley, 1989.

[Stroustrup 91] Stroustrup, B. J., *The C++ Programming Language*. New York: Prentice-Hall, 1991.

[Smith 90] Smith, Jerry D., *Reusability & Software Construction in C & C++*. New York: John Wiley & Sons, 1990.

[Weiner 90] Weiner, Richard, and Pinson, Lewis, *Object-Oriented Programming in C++*. Reading, MA: Addison-Wesley, 1989.

■ OTHER

[Kernighan 84] Kernighan, Brian W., and Pike, Rob, *The UNIX Programming Environment*. New York: Prentice-Hall, 1984.

[Lindley 90] Lindley, Craig A., *Practical Image Processing in C*. New York: John Wiley & Sons, 1990.

INDEX